MONEY IN YOUR POCKET

MONEY IN YOUR POCKET

PAUL N. STRASSELS

CONTROL DATA PUBLISHING

MINNEAPOLIS, MINNESOTA

1981

MONEY IN YOUR POCKET
by Paul N. Strassels

Editor: Pamela Espeland
Design: Koechel/Peterson Design
Index: Mary Rockcastle

Library of Congress Cataloging in Publication Data

Strassels, Paul N.
  Money in your pocket.

  Includes index.
  1. Tax planning—United States. I. Title.
KF6297.s8   343.7304   81–15098
ISBN 0–89893–507–5   347.3034   AACR2

Dedication

To Herbert Cohen,
who taught me
I had options

"Taxes are what we pay for a
civilized society."
> U.S. Supreme Court Chief Justice
> Oliver Wendell Holmes

"There is nothing sinister in arranging one's affairs to keep taxes as low as possible. Nobody owes any public duty to pay more than the law demands."

> Appeals Court Judge
> Learned Hand

Acknowledgments

I must express my sincere thanks and appreciation to a very special group of people who have been so instrumental in producing this book.

To my brother, James H. Strassels, who encouraged me to begin this project in the first place.

To James Martin, who handled a great deal of the detailed tax research.

To Anne V. Tuthill, who did all of my typing and retyping efficiently and well.

To Lois M. Coltrin, who patiently handled all of the day-to-day details of this project. Her copyediting and rewriting talents were invaluable.

And, finally, to Pamela Espeland, who had the toughness to deal with a project of this depth in such a short period of time. Her editing skills made this book what it is.

P.N.S.

CONTENTS

(III continued)

[x]

FOREWORD

Everyone is feeling the money pinch these days. Inflation is devouring salary raises. Medical costs are soaring. So are the prices of new clothes, cars, gasoline, heating fuel, food, and housing. Interest rates are sky-high—and so are taxes.

Despite the tax cuts that were built into President Ronald Reagan's Economic Recovery Tax Act of 1981, your taxes are still rising. (The Tax Act didn't lower your taxes, no matter what you may have heard; it just slowed their rate of increase.) What can you do to make things easier on yourself?

You can stop overpaying your income taxes. If you're like most people, you're probably paying more than you really owe. Why? Because you're not taking advantage of dozens—maybe hundreds—of *legal* tax breaks.

Let me get something straight at the very beginning. I believe in paying taxes. Personally, I pay my fair share. But I don't pay more than the law requires me to. Instead, I plan my taxes very carefully, year after year. I consider the tax effect of every financial decision I make. I pay attention to the changes in the tax law.

You should, too.

This doesn't require an extraordinary amount of effort. You don't need to be a tax wizard or a financial genius in order to get your taxes down to a more reasonable, manageable level. You don't have to hire a full-time tax accountant or attorney.

You *do* have to be willing to change your attitude about your taxes, though. And you *do* have to start taking an active, positive approach to handling your own money and tax affairs.

Over the past three years, I've appeared on hundreds of television and radio shows. I've answered thousands of tax questions from viewers and listeners. Along the way, I've discovered that a lot of people are simply uninformed about their taxes. And what they don't know is hurting them.

MONEY IN YOUR POCKET has been written in response to the questions people have asked me most frequently. It isn't a tax manual. It isn't meant to be the last word for everyone in every financial circumstance. It can't be all things to all people. For example, don't look here for advice on state and local tax issues—you won't find it. These tips are aimed primarily at helping you to lower your *federal* income taxes, where most of your tax money goes each year.

If you earn between $15,000 and $100,000 a year and you're tired of paying too much in taxes, MONEY IN YOUR POCKET is for you. Not every tax tip in this book will benefit you directly; in fact, there will probably be some that don't apply to you at all. But I know that, on the whole, you'll come out ahead if only a handful do.

Wealthy people aren't the only ones who have tax breaks coming to them. However, they're often the only ones who know how to use them. I hope that this book will change that. I want *you* to start holding on to more of your hard-earned dollars. I want *you* to avoid some of the traps that unwary taxpayers often fall into.

And, most important, I want *you* to be your own best financial advisor—beginning today.

Paul Strassels
Northern Virginia
November, 1981

I.

MAKING THE NEW TAX LAWS WORK FOR YOU

The rules of the tax game have changed. President Ronald Reagan's Economic Recovery Tax Act of 1981 has already had an effect on your wallet, and you'll be feeling it more in the months and years to come.

There's a whole new set of tax laws to deal with. Some of these laws will cost you money. But some of them can save you a bundle—if you know what to do with them. With a little knowledge and planning, you *can* take advantage of the new tax laws and make them work for you.

Lower Individual Tax Rates

For most people, the best piece of news to come out of the 1981 Economic Recovery Tax Act is the reduction in the tax rates.

These rate cuts apply all across the board—to upper and lower income taxpayers alike. It's no secret that they'll do the most good for people in the highest brackets, but even those who don't make a lot of money will benefit over the next few years.

On October 1, 1981, the withholding tax rates were lowered by 5 percent. On July 1, 1982, they go down another 10 percent. And on July 1, 1983, they drop by still another 10 percent.

There is a corresponding reduction in the overall tax rates. This means that your tax liability will be lower in the future than it would have been without the new law. You'll pay less taxes on the same amount of income.

Example: For 1982, a single person with no dependents who earns $20,000 a year and doesn't itemize will pay $350–$400 less in federal income taxes because of the change in the rates.

On the other hand, a married couple with two children, a combined income of $20,000, and Schedule A deductions amounting to 20 percent of their income will save only about $200 on their federal income taxes. (That's right. Married people won't get as big a break as single people.) If that same couple has a combined income of $50,000, they'll pay $850 less in taxes. And if they earn $70,000, they'll take home an extra $1,600.

Of course, these are only averages. Everyone's personal situation is bound to be a little different.

You're probably wondering what these lower rates mean for the 1981 tax year. The answer is: not a whole lot. If you're single and earning $20,000, the October 1 cuts put about $50 in your pocket. If you're married with the same income, make that $25.

Beginning in 1982, taxpayers in the higher income brackets can start enjoying another tax break as well. The top tax rate for individuals drops to 50 percent. This applies to all types of income, both earned and unearned. Through 1981, unearned income (like dividends and interest) could be taxed at rates as high as 70 percent. But no more.

The maximum rate will stay at that 50 percent level. In other words, no matter how much money you bring in, the government will never be able to lay claim to more than half of it (and probably much less).

The amount of income you'll be able to earn before moving into the highest tax bracket will also go up. If you're single, your 1981 taxes are subject to the 50 percent marginal rate if your taxable income is $35,000. That figure jumps to $41,500 for 1982 and $55,300 for 1983. If you're married filing jointly, you're in the 50 percent marginal bracket for 1981 if your combined taxable income is $48,000. For 1982, you'll be able to earn $85,000 before finding yourself in that bracket; for 1983, $110,000.

Note: Even with the tax cuts, you'll still pay more income taxes for 1981 than you did for 1980. And your 1982 tax bill will probably be even higher. In other words, the new laws won't lower your taxes—they'll just reduce their rate of increase. Your taxes will keep going up, but a bit more slowly. That's some solace.

The Marriage Penalty

It's increasingly common these days for both husbands and wives to hold down jobs. Many families need two incomes to get by or get ahead a little. And more and more women are choosing to work outside the home.

Almost everyone knows that an employed married couple filing jointly pays higher taxes than the same two people would if they weren't married. Over the past few years, there's been a lot of controversy surrounding the so-called "marriage penalty." Here's the way things stand now:

1. President Reagan's Economic Recovery Tax Act made changes in the tax rules concerning the marriage penalty. These take effect January 1, 1982. They are *not* retroactive. In other words, you don't get any tax relief on your 1981 return.

2. The marriage penalty has been eased, but not eliminated.

a. Married couples with two incomes get a tax break beginning with their 1982 returns. To qualify, they must file jointly.

b. For 1982 only, the tax break for two-income families is limited to $1,500 or 5 percent of the secondary income, whichever is less.

c. For 1983, the tax break for two-income families is

limited to $3,000 or 10 percent of the secondary income, whichever is less.

Example: In 1981, Carol and Jim Ferris earned $15,000 and $30,000, respectively. They get no tax relief from the marriage penalty when they file their 1981 return.

(To simplify this example, let's assume that their incomes stay the same over the next two years.)

For 1982, Carol and Jim can take a $750 deduction on their joint return—5 percent of her $15,000 income.

For 1983, they can take a $1,500 deduction—10 percent of $15,000.

The 10 percent deduction will apply until the secondary income jumps above $30,000, after which their deduction will be limited to $3,000.

Caution: For tax purposes, your marital status as of December 31 determines how the IRS views you for the entire preceding year. In other words, if you get married on December 31, you'll be saddled with the marriage penalty—just as if you'd been married all year. It doesn't seem fair, but it's the law.

Some people think that they can avoid paying the marriage penalty by getting divorced on December 31, remarrying early in January, and getting divorced again the following December 31. They're wrong; the IRS won't recognize the tax effect of this kind of planning.

Review Your Estate Plans NOW

The 1981 Economic Recovery Tax Act made some changes in the tax law that will affect the way everyone, repeat everyone, should handle their estate plans. If you've done any estate planning in the past—if you had a will drawn up, or made provisions for the transfer of your assets to your spouse, your children, or your favorite charity, or established one or more trusts—then I urge you to call your attorney today. Make an appointment to review your current estate plans in light of the new laws.

There are three major changes to keep in mind:

1. As of January 1, 1982, husbands and wives can make

unlimited transfers of money and property among themselves.

This wasn't true in the past. What it means is that you'll want to rethink the way you and your spouse own your property, whether you hold it jointly or separately.

2. Also beginning in January, the estate tax exemption increases.

For tax year 1981, the exemption is $175,625. Under the new law, more and larger estates will go untaxed. Here's the way things look for the future: For 1982, the exemption jumps to $225,000; for 1983, $275,000; for 1984, $325,000; for 1985, $400,000; for 1986, $500,000; and for 1987, $600,000.

3. Finally, the maximum tax *rate* on any portion of an estate that exceeds the limit drops, too.

For 1981, the top tax rate on estates is 70 percent. For 1982, it drops by 5 points to 65 percent, and it continues to fall 5 points a year for the next three years. In other words, the 1983 maximum rate is pegged at 60 percent; for 1984, it's 55 percent; and for 1985, it's 50 percent, where it's supposed to remain.

Which estates get saddled with the maximum tax rate? For 1982, those valued at $4 million. That figure becomes $3.5 million in 1983, $3 million in 1984, and $2.5 million in 1985, the point at which it should level off.

Estate planning can be time-consuming simply because there are so many variables to consider. But don't procrastinate! With the 1981 tax law changes, estate planning should become a top priority for you and your entire family.

Tax-Free Gifts

For years, the IRS has allowed you to give money to your friends and relatives—as long as you didn't give them too much. If your generosity exceeded a certain amount, though, the tax collector got involved. Thanks to the recent changes in the tax law, you can start making much larger gifts without having to report them.

The old rule (effective until December 31, 1981) stated that you could give as much as $3,000 in cash or property to as many people as you wanted to without having to file a gift tax return. If, for example, there were four people you felt like being nice to, you could pass along $3,000 to each of them for a total of $12,000. You just couldn't give any one person more than $3,000 without reporting it.

Husband-wife teams could make joint gifts of $6,000 per person per year. Again, they couldn't give any one person more than that without having to report it.

The new rule (effective January 1, 1982) raises the $3,000 ceiling to $10,000 and the $6,000 ceiling to $20,000. You can give away these amounts to as many people as you want. For tax purposes, it may not be wise to give any one person more than the limit.

The change is a good one, and it was long overdue. Before Congress approved it, the IRS was getting into the picture when parents paid $5,000 in tuition, room, and board for a child in college or bought a kid a car as a graduation present. The higher limits of $10,000 and $20,000 make sense in today's world.

By the way, these rules apply only to gifts you give to family members and friends—not to charitable organizations. If you make donations to charity, you should claim them as tax deductions on your Schedule A.

Reporting Interest and Dividend Income

There have been major changes in the tax law regarding how much dividend and interest income you have to report and pay taxes on.

Recall that for tax year 1980, you had to report all of your taxable interest income. When it came to dividends, you were supposed to list all of them, but you may have been able to exclude up to $100 ($200 for married couples filing jointly).

For tax year 1981, the rules change. You're supposed to add up all your taxable interest income and all your dividend income and then total the two. You may be able to exclude up to $200 of this combined income ($400 for married couples filing jointly).

Of course, not all dividends and interest qualify for this $200/$400 exclusion. The easiest way to find out exactly how much of yours do (and how much do not) is to look very carefully at the 1099-INT (for interest) and 1099-DIV (for dividends) forms or other statements you receive from the companies and financial institutions you have accounts with. Each slip will show you:

1. how much dividend or interest income you received during the year from a particular company or financial institution;

2. how much of the income qualifies for the $200/$400 exclusion; and

3. how much does not qualify.

Note: For tax year 1982, the old 1980 rules go back into effect. In other words, you'll have to report all of your taxable interest income and all of your dividends. And the amount of dividends you may be able to exclude will again be $100/$200.

But for now, here's how to report your 1981 dividend and interest income:

1. If you file the long form, and if your interest income (line 8a) for the year was $400 or less *and* your dividend income (line 8b) was $400 or less, you can simply report the totals on the front of your 1040.

2. If you file the long form, and if your interest income was more than $400, you'll have to fill out Schedule B and attach it to your return. On Schedule B, you'll list the amounts of interest you received and the companies that paid it to you.

The same goes for your dividend income.

Example: You earned $350 in dividends and $800 in interest during 1981. List your dividends on the front of your 1040. Then fill out Schedule B for your interest income (since it amounted to more than $400) and attach it to your return before you mail it in.

In past years, you had to file the long form if either your dividends or your interest income came to more than $400. But for 1981, you can file the short form, 1040A, even if the amount of interest and the amount of dividends you received both exceeded the $400 limit. There's a place on the back of the 1040A where you can list the amounts and the companies that paid them to you.

Caution: Credit unions pay interest income to savers, even though many designate their payouts as "dividends." And those high-yielding money market mutual funds pay dividends, not interest. This distinction is especially important if you're approaching the $400 reporting ceilings.

A final reminder: If you do file Schedule B, be sure to answer the questions in Part III pertaining to foreign accounts and trusts. You have to answer them even if they don't apply to you.

Reporting the Profits from the Sale of Your Home

The IRS wants to know all about any money that comes your way. If you sell your home and profit from the deal, you can bet they'll be interested in hearing about it.

Two recent changes in the tax law can benefit you when it's time to report the gain on the sale of your personal residence:

1. If you sold your home at a profit on or after January 21, 1980 (or are in the process of selling it now), the law now gives you two full years to replace it with a more costly one so you can defer paying taxes on your gain.

That's good news. In the past, you had only 18 months in which to accomplish this. If you took any longer, you had to declare your profits on your tax return, usually in the form of a long-term capital gain. Just remember the key date: January 21, 1980.

2. If you're 55 or older and you sold your personal residence on or after July 21, 1981, you may be able to pocket up to $125,000 of your profits tax-free. That's a substantial increase over the previous limit of $100,000.

Caution: There are other restrictions that still apply to people 55 and older who want to sell their homes without paying taxes on their profits. For example, you must use your home as your primary residence for at least three out of five years prior to its sale. And you can't sell it before your 55th birthday.

Lower Taxes on Capital Gains

One of the nicer side benefits to come out of the 1981 Economic Recovery Tax Act is the reduced tax rate on capital gains income.

For capital assets sold on or after June 10, 1981, the maximum tax rate is 20 percent of the profits. (It's lower for people who aren't in the top income tax brackets.) The old maximum rate—which applies to those assets sold prior to June 10, 1981—was 28 percent. The 8 percent difference can mean a sizable tax savings for investors.

Example: You're in a high income tax bracket, and in July, 1981, you sold a piece of real estate at a $40,000 profit. If you still had to compute your taxes on this gain at the old rate, your tax bill for 1981 would be increased by $11,200 ($40,000 × 28 percent).

But because you made the sale after June 9, 1981, you get to use the new rate, and your tax increase is $8,000 ($40,000 × 20 percent). In effect, your taxes have been cut by $3,200.

The reduced tax rate on long-term capital gains wasn't written into the Tax Act. But it came about because of something that was. As part of the Tax Act, Congress lowered the highest tax bracket for individuals from 70 percent to 50 percent. And that in turn lowered the capital gains tax rate.

I don't want to go into too much detail here, but I will briefly explain how this all works.

If you own a piece of investment property for more than a year (that is, a minimum of one year and one day) before selling it, you can pocket 60 percent of your profit tax-free. The other 40 percent is taxed.

Your capital gains tax rate is a function of this 40 percent multiplied by your marginal tax bracket percentage. If you're in the top tax bracket, that used to work out to 28 percent (40 percent × 70 percent). But now, thanks to the Tax Act, it's 20 percent (40 percent × 50 percent).

The All Savers Certificate

The All Savers Certificate has received more publicity and caused more confusion than anything else in the entire 1981 Economic Recovery Tax Act. Before you invest in one, you should know the facts.

The All Savers is a one-year certificate of deposit (CD). Its most appealing feature is that the interest it earns is tax-free, up to a maximum of $1,000 for single taxpayers and $2,000 for married couples filing jointly. The interest rate for these CDs is relatively high—70 percent of the current *investment* rate on 52-week treasury securities. (Don't worry about figuring out this rate; your banker will do it for you.)

Even though the All Savers is attractive, it isn't for everyone. In order to get the most out of one, you'll need to invest a sizable chunk of money. And once you do, you won't be able to touch it for a year—not unless you want to pay a heavy premature withdrawal penalty and sacrifice your tax break.

The $1,000 or $2,000 in tax-free interest is a *one time only* exclusion. You can buy as many All Savers CDs as you want, but any interest they earn over and above your limit will be fully taxed.

Here's a simple formula you can use to find out the top investment you should make in an All Savers at any given interest rate:

1. Take the maximum amount of tax-free interest you're allowed ($1,000 or $2,000), and

2. Divide it by the All Savers rate provided by your banker.

Example: You're married and file a joint return. The present All Savers rate is 12.00 percent. Divide the $2,000 in tax-free interest you can earn by .1200, and you'll get $16,667. That's the most you can invest and still realize a tax savings.

What if you want to purchase an All Savers but don't have the cash available? You can borrow the money to pay for it. Just keep in mind that the interest you pay on the loan will *not* be deductible later on. According to the IRS, any interest paid on money borrowed for the purpose of investing in tax-exempt securities doesn't qualify for the Schedule A interest deduction.

Financial institutions began offering All Savers on October 1, 1981 and will continue to sell them until December 31, 1982. If you buy one, plan ahead for what you'll do with your funds when the CD matures. Chances are you won't want to invest them in another All Savers Certificate.

Individual Retirement Accounts (IRAs)—1982

Today it's worthwhile for everyone to think about Individual Retirement Accounts (IRAs). In the past, you weren't allowed to open an IRA if you worked for a company that offered a tax-qualified retirement plan. And even if you could have an IRA, your maximum contribution was limited to $1,500 or 15 percent of your salary, whichever was smaller.

As of January 1, 1982, these rules change. Thanks to the Economic Recovery Tax Act of 1981, you can now establish and fund your own IRA regardless of whether you're covered by a company pension plan. The only real eligibility requirement is that you have a job of some kind.

In addition, you can now contribute as much as $2,000 into your IRA for 1982, as long as you make at least that much. The old 15 percent earnings limitation has been removed. In other words, if you work part time and earn only $1,000 or $2,000, you can contribute—and deduct—100 percent of your earnings. Married couples with only one wage earner may set up "spousal IRAs," one for each partner, and contribute up to $2,250 divided between the two accounts.

Where can you open an IRA? Most banks, savings and loans, and credit unions offer them. Some insurance companies have them, as do many mutual funds. Shop around before you decide where to park your IRA money. Personally, I prefer an account that allows me to direct the way in which my money is invested. Many financial institutions don't provide this option. Brokers and mutual funds often do.

An IRA can result in a tax savings to you, but it can also

cost you plenty if you're not careful. Both the IRS and banking institutions impose certain restrictions on your account.

Under the tax law, any money you put into an IRA is effectively tied up by the IRS until you reach the age of 59½. If you want to cash in your account before then, you'll have to pay the IRS a nondeductible 6 percent premature withdrawal penalty. You'll also have to declare the amount you receive as income on your tax return.

There is an exception to this rule: If you die or become disabled before you turn 59½, the money may be removed from your account and the IRS won't charge a penalty. The financial institution may, though, if the account has not yet matured.

Transferring an IRA can cause problems, too. The IRS usually won't mind, but the financial institution where you originally funded the plan may charge you a stiff premature withdrawal penalty.

Example: You have an IRA at your local financial institution. You have invested your funds in a 30-month certificate of deposit (CD) at a high interest rate. You move to another state, and you want to take your IRA with you and reestablish it at a bank near your new home.

In the eyes of the IRS, you can transfer your account as long as the funds aren't actually made available to you. But the financial institution that first held your IRA may saddle you with a premature withdrawal penalty on the CD.

How can you avoid this penalty? By leaving your money where it is and not paying any more into this account. Then, when the CD matures, you can transfer these funds at no cost to you. In the meantime, you can always open up another IRA somewhere else.

That's something most people don't realize. There's no law saying that you can have only one IRA. In fact, you can have two or three or as many as you want, as long as your total contribution for 1982 doesn't exceed $2,000.

Caution: Because of the 1981 Economic Recovery Tax Act, you have to keep two sets of rules in mind when thinking about IRAs—one for 1981, and another for 1982. (See

Chapter II for the 1981 rules.) A simple, innocent mixup between the two years could cost you money.

Charity and Nonitemizers

Approximately 40 percent of all taxpayers file the short form, 1040A. The rest file the long form, 1040. Even if you file the long form, you may not have enough deductions to itemize on Schedule A. And if you don't itemize, you never get the chance to deduct your charitable contributions.

This doesn't change for tax year 1981. However, beginning with your 1982 return, you can take advantage of a small tax break that will compensate for at least part of your generosity.

Here's the rule:

For 1982, you can deduct from your gross income 25 percent of the first $100 you give to charity. That amounts to a grand total of $25.

This limit applies to both single taxpayers and married couples. If you're married and file separately, you and your spouse can claim a maximum of $12.50 each.

You're right—it isn't much. Frankly, I don't think this tax break deserved all of the publicity it received when the 1981 Economic Recovery Tax Act was signed into law. But it's something, and you shouldn't ignore it if you can take it.

The future looks a little brighter.

Although the same $25 ceiling applies for the 1983 tax year, it rises to 25 percent of the first $300 for 1984, or $75. For 1985 it jumps again, this time to 50 percent of your total contributions—no more $300 limit. And for 1986 even the 50 percent maximum expires, and you can deduct the entire value of your charitable giving, just as if you were itemizing on Schedule A.

Don't get used to this new and improved deduction, though. For 1987, things go back to the way they were in 1981. Nonitemizers get no tax break.

The Child and Dependent Care Credit

It's difficult for working parents to find child care facilities that they feel are right for their children. And the cost of a good day care center or sitter makes it even harder. Luckily, the IRS recognizes this in the form of a tax break.

If you pay someone to take care of your children so you can hold down a job or go to school, you can deduct a portion of these costs on your tax return. Simply fill out IRS Form 2441, Credit for Child and Dependent Care Expenses, and attach it to your 1040. (You'll have to file the long form if you want to take this tax credit.)

How large can your credit be? For 1981, you can claim up to 20 percent of the first $2,000 you spend on child care costs for one child. For two or more children, this figure rises to $4,000. This means a maximum tax credit for you of $400 or $800, depending on how many children you have.

As part of the 1981 Economic Recovery Tax Act, Congress has approved an even bigger child care credit for 1982. The $2,000 and $4,000 limits are upped to $2,400 and $4,800. And you may be able to claim a greater percentage of your child care costs than you could on your 1981 return, especially if you're in a lower income bracket.

If your adjusted gross income for 1982 is under $10,000, you can take a tax credit in the amount of 30 percent of your child care expenses. This credit drops one percentage point for every $2,000 you earn above $10,000 and finally levels off at $28,000.

Example: If your adjusted gross income for 1982 is $18,000, you can deduct 26 percent of your child care costs. In other words, if you have one child and spend the $2,400 limit, you can take a $624 credit. If you have two or more children and your costs total $4,800, you can take a credit of $1,248.

If your adjusted gross income is over $28,000, you can still claim 20 percent of your child care expenses.

This credit also applies to the care of dependents other than children.

Example: Your elderly father lives with you and needs

constant attention. In order for you to go to work each day, you must hire someone to come in and attend to him. The credit is yours for the taking.

What if you become ill or meet with an accident that leaves you at home in need of care? Your husband or wife may hire someone to come into your home while he or she works or goes to school. And you can write off part of the costs.

Even if you send your kids to summer camp so you can keep working, you may be able to claim some of the camp fees.

You're entitled to the child and dependent care credit regardless of whether you work full or part time, are self-employed, or are actively looking for a job.

Adoption Expenses: A New Deduction

Anyone who has ever adopted a child knows how exhausting the process can be. The mountains of paperwork, the long waits, and the high costs can take their toll. Fortunately, the aggravation doesn't stop many people from adopting children who need homes.

Until now, the IRS has not been very sympathetic to adoptive parents. They have consistently ruled that adoption expenses are personal and therefore not tax deductible. But thanks to the Economic Recovery Tax Act of 1981, this situation may be changing for the better.

You may now be able to deduct expenses relating to the adoption of a so-called "hard-to-place" child. Translated, this usually refers to a minority child or one who is handicapped.

This deduction applies to any expenses incurred after December 31, 1980, so you can take advantage of it on your 1981 return. If you're currently involved in adopting a child and some of your costs are paid as of December 31, 1981, you may be able to deduct them as well.

To qualify for this deduction, you will have to file the long form and itemize on Schedule A. Claim your costs under "miscellaneous deductions."

There are two important restrictions to be aware of:

1. Your deduction is limited to a maximum of $1,500; and

2. You can only deduct what the law terms "reasonable and necessary" adoption fees, attorneys' fees, court costs, and other expenses directly relating to a legal adoption.

The "reasonable and necessary" rule may mean that some of your expenses aren't deductible. My advice is to go ahead and claim what you think is fair. You deserve as much as you can get of this deduction.

Good News for Small Businesses

The 1981 Economic Recovery Tax Act provides some relief for small businesses. Not a lot, but some. And considering the high taxes and mountains of paperwork involved in running a small business, any change for the better is bound to be welcome.

For the most part, you'll have to make do with the old tax laws when you file your 1981 return. But beginning with tax year 1982, you'll be able to take advantage of several new rules:

1. The corporate tax rate drops.

For 1982, the rate on the first $25,000 of taxable income falls to 17 percent (down one point from 18 percent). It drops again, to 16 percent, for 1983.

The rate on the next $25,000 of taxable income—20 percent for 1981— becomes 19 percent for 1982 and 18 percent for 1983.

2. The allowable retained earnings and profits level rises.

For 1982, your small business can accumulate as much as $250,000 in earnings and profits before the IRS will question your need for this much capital—*unless* your business is a personal service corporation operating in the fields of health, law, engineering, architecture, accounting, actuarial science, consulting, or the performing arts, in which case the old $150,000 limit will still apply.

3. Subchapter S corporations can have more shareholders.

As of 1982, the special Subchapter S corporations used

by many small businesses can have as many as 25 share-holders. That's up from 15.

Another change included in the Tax Act has to do with depreciation deductions. This change is retroactive to January 1, 1981, which means that you can benefit from it on your 1981 return.

At one time or another, most small business owners, their accountants, and the IRS have all been at odds with one another over the issue of depreciation deductions. That's because no one has ever bothered to spell out exactly how these deductions should be taken. But Congress has now solved that problem. They've made precise determinations as to how much depreciation can be claimed on a business car or truck, a building, office equipment, and so forth. And they've established schedules you can use when depreciating your business assets.

How will that affect you? To begin with, it will make your tax computations a little easier. But more importantly, it will give you and your accountant plenty of ammunition in the event of an IRS audit.

It's a well-known fact that the IRS tends to audit small business owners rather heavily. That's because—according to IRS statistics—small business has the lowest level of voluntary compliance with the tax law. One reason for these unflattering statistics has been the ongoing dispute over depreciation deductions. Whenever a small business owner made a claim, an IRS auditor could almost always find something wrong with it and assess more taxes.

But no more. If you follow the new rules when depreciating your business assets, the IRS will have to accept what you put down on your business return. This should result in fewer IRS audits and less expense to you for your accountant's time.

New Rules for Business Gifts and Awards

Thanks to the 1981 Economic Recovery Tax Act, your employer can now be more generous when it comes to giving certain types of gifts and awards.

In the past, employers were limited to a maximum $25 deduction for business gifts made to individuals during the year. There was one very important exception to this rule: They were allowed to deduct as much as $100 for awards made for length of service or safety achievement.

They're still restricted to the $25 deduction for gifts in general—like holiday turkeys, for example. But the $100 limit on awards has been upped to $400. And a third qualifying category has been added: productivity.

If you're a worthy employee, in other words, then you might receive a pleasant surprise one of these days. You might get that gold watch at retirement after all. The new rule took effect August 13, 1981—the day the Tax Act was signed into law—so awards made during the latter part of 1981 are covered by it.

Don't worry about reporting your award on your income tax return. Your employer should take care of this for you by including it under "other income" on your W-2.

Recommendation: If you're an employer and you want to make extra nice gifts to your employees this year, be sure to designate them as awards for productivity, length of service, or safety achievement. Then go ahead and splurge to the tune of $400 each—and deduct the entire amount from your income on your business return.

What if you're self-employed? You may even be able to give yourself a $400 award and write it off at tax time.

II.
FIGURING YOUR INCOME

The IRS wants to know all about your income. They'll haggle with you over questionable deductions and credits, but when it comes to your income, they want the facts.

The tax law defines your gross income as "all income from whatever source derived." This sounds as if you must report every penny you earn. However, some income is tax-free, pure and simple. Some is tax-free under certain circumstances. And tax-free income doesn't have to be reported.

By reporting only that which the law requires you to, you may be able to reduce your tax bill—safely and legally.

Some Income Is Tax-Free

The IRS would like you to think that you have to report all of your income. According to the definition in the tax law, "Income is income from whatever source derived." And, in general, income is taxed. But there are some types that are actually nontaxable. Like the following:

- Social security and Medicare benefits
- Your federal income tax refund
- Proceeds you receive as a beneficiary on a life insurance policy

- An inheritance (for federal tax purposes; you may end up paying state or local inheritance taxes)
- Child support payments you receive
- Workmen's compensation
- Funds you receive from agencies for the care of a foster child
- Money you get from coworkers you car-pool with
- A cash rebate for the purchase of a new car
- Small year-end gifts from your employer, such as a holiday ham or a pen and pencil set (as long as it's valued at under $25)
- Gifts of money you receive from your friends and relatives

There's more: If you're 55 years old or older and you sell your personal residence, you can pocket as much as $125,000 of your profits tax-free. If you invest in an All Savers Certificate, the first $1,000 in interest it earns is nontaxable ($2,000 if you're married filing jointly).

If you borrow some money, you don't have to pay taxes on the amount of the loan.

Most of the income you receive during the year does have to be reported to the IRS. But some doesn't. If you're in doubt about something, you should check it out. You may be pleasantly surprised.

You Can't Assign Away Your Income

It would be nice if you could assign away some of your income by shifting it around to other members of your family—like your young children, your retired parents, or someone else who's in a lower tax bracket than you are. Then you could avoid paying income taxes on all of it yourself.

But you can't run away from income that rightfully belongs to you. If you earn it, you're supposed to report it and pay taxes on it. The law simply won't allow you to manipulate your tax bill in this way.

Example: You're under contract to a local business. You consider asking them to make out your last two monthly checks to your children instead of to you. It sounds like a good setup—and nobody would ever know the difference. Right?

Wrong. It just won't work.

Note: If you hold off on billing the business, you can *delay* these checks until early 1982. Then you won't have to report the income until you file your 1982 return.

You can give some of your *assets* away, if you want to. And that will result in a tax break of sorts.

Example: You own some stock that pays dividends. In an effort to cut your taxes, you decide to give the stock to your daughter. Once you do this, the dividend income and tax responsibility will be hers, not yours. But you will no longer have control over the stock. It's up to you to determine if the trade-off is worth it.

Don't Pay Taxes on Someone Else's Interest Income

Many parents have joint bank accounts with their children. However, most don't realize that these accounts can cost them extra tax dollars if they're not set up properly.

Example: You go to your local bank to open a joint savings account for your young daughter. When the new-accounts clerk asks for your social security number, you dutifully supply it.

Early the following year, you receive a Form 1099 from your bank telling you how much interest the account earned through December 31. (The IRS gets a copy of the same statement.) You include the interest in your income when preparing your tax return and pay taxes on it.

What you may not be aware of is that you can easily—and *legally*—avoid paying taxes on this interest income. How? By getting a social security number for your daughter and then placing the account under *her* number. This means that an individual return *may* have to be filed for her at tax time. But since she'll probably be in a lower tax bracket than you, your family will realize an overall tax savings.

Here's the rule that determines whether or not a return will have to be filed for your daughter: If her *total* unearned income for the year is $1,000 or more, then the return will be due. If it's less than that amount, it won't be necessary to file—although it may be a good idea to do so anyway.

When you change the account from your social security number to your daughter's, you're acknowledging that the account is legally hers. In other words, you cannot use any of the funds in it for your own benefit, or even to satisfy your obligation to support your daughter. As long as you don't touch the money, you can continue to list the account under her number and avoid paying taxes on the interest.

All the IRS cares about is whose number the account appears under. They'll look for that number on the 1099 they receive from your bank.

What if your bank has already reported the interest income to the IRS under your social security number? Chances are that the IRS will match this report against your tax return. When they find that you haven't included this interest in your income, they'll send you a letter asking why.

If this happens, simply write them back and explain that:

1. the income was improperly reported under your social security number;

2. the income actually belongs to your child; and

3. the income was reported on your child's personal individual income tax return. (It may not have been necessary to file one, but if you did, this will serve as backup for your claim.)

If you hold other joint accounts with your children—such as checking accounts that earn interest, trusts, or securities accounts—you may want to change the way they're listed, too. Then you won't have to pay taxes on the interest or dividends they earn.

Note: You can change the way a joint account is listed at almost any time. Just tell your banker that you want it done.

When Your State Tax Refund Is Income—
and When It Isn't

Most people don't have any trouble figuring out their income and listing it on their tax returns. Salary, wage, dividend, and interest income are usually fairly straightforward. However, reporting last year's tax refunds as part of this year's income can get confusing.

Here's the good news: A *federal* income tax refund is *always* tax-free. In other words, you never have to include a federal refund as part of your gross income on your federal return.

State and local tax refunds are another matter, though. If you received a refund last spring or summer from your state or county government, you *may* have to list it as income on line 9 of your 1040 and pay tax on it.

Dig out copies of your state and federal income tax returns for 1980. Look first at your state return. Did it call for a refund? If so, look next at your federal return and answer this all-important question:

Did you itemize your deductions on Schedule A?

If you *did not,* then any state or local refund you received in 1981 is tax-free. You don't have to report it to the IRS on your 1981 federal return.

If you *did* itemize, and if you included in your itemized deductions the amounts that were withheld from your paychecks for state and local taxes (any and all quarterly estimated payments you made to the state, and/or any additional taxes you had to pay when you filed your 1980 return), then you'll have to report your state refund as part of your income on this year's 1040.

What if, in the past, you inadvertently reported and paid taxes on state and local refunds when you really shouldn't have? My advice is to file an amended return on Form 1040X for each year you want to change. The IRS will send you an additional refund, plus interest.

Unemployment Compensation

As unfair as it seems, all or part of a person's unemployment compensation benefits may be taxed. If you lost your job last year and collected unemployment, you'll probably get an information slip (IRS Form 1099-UC) in the mail showing the total amount you received in 1981. As part of the IRS's document matching program, they'll compare this figure to what you list on your return. They'll want to make sure that you haven't forgotten to report your benefits—if you have to. Not everyone does.

How can you figure out how much of your benefits, if any, will be taxed? Follow the step-by-step instructions in the IRS's tax package. (If you didn't receive a tax package in the mail, get one from your local IRS office.)

In general, single taxpayers can receive as much as $20,000 in wages, interest, and other income (including unemployment compensation) before the IRS will be interested in taxing any of their unemployment benefits. Married couples filing jointly can take in as much as $25,000.

If your income exceeds the limit, though, you have a little figuring to do. Basically, the IRS requires you to report as taxable unemployment compensation either half of your income over the limit, or the total amount of your unemployment compensation, whichever is less.

Example: If you're single and made $24,000 last year, including $3,000 in unemployment benefits, then you must report $2,000 of the $4,000 you made above the $20,000 ceiling. (This is less than the $3,000 in benefits you received.) But if that $24,000 figure included only $300 in benefits, *all* of your unemployment is taxable.

Prizes and Awards

Don't be too envious of all those game show contestants who win fabulous prizes. There's something the announcers aren't telling you: Those prizes are taxed.

That's right. If you get lucky—if you have the winning ticket, or your name is drawn out of the hat for the sweepstakes, or you answer all the questions on the big board—it could cost you a bundle in extra taxes.

Under the law, you are required to include in your income any money and/or property you receive in the form of awards or prizes. This amount goes on line 20, "other income," of the long form, 1040. (You must file the long form in order to report awards and prizes; there's no place to do this on the 1040A.)

There are a few exceptions to this rule. You don't have to report a gift from your company for a special occasion (like a holiday ham or turkey), *if* it isn't cash and *if* its value is under $25.

A genuine gift is tax-free to you. For example, if your uncle gives you a $2,000 wedding present, you don't have to pay taxes on it.

An inheritance you receive is also tax-free to you (for federal tax purposes, at least). So are some scholarships, fellowships, and educational grants.

If you are honored with an award in recognition of a past accomplishment (usually in a religious, charitable, scientific, artistic, educational, literary, or civic field), *and* you didn't have to perform any specific action in order to get it, *and* your future services aren't required as a result, you don't have to report It.

However, anything you win in a drawing or on a television or radio quiz show must be included. Money and prizes you win in a beauty contest are taxable. So are fishing derby, lottery, and raffle winnings. Employee bonuses and outstanding work awards, holiday season cash bonuses, company-furnished vacations, and a company car given as a performance award—these are taxable, too.

Prizes and awards can cause real tax headaches. If you win something other than cash, it's up to you to figure out what it's worth. In the case of a car, determine the fair market value. For a vacation or a trip, call a travel agent and ask about ticket and accommodation prices. What about a work of art? That's more difficult.

In general, you should be as reasonable and honest as

possible. Don't undervalue your winnings, but don't overvalue them either.

It may be hard to come up with the cash to pay the taxes on an especially big prize. It's great to win a $100,000 house—until you discover that it's going to cost you an extra $40,000 or so in income taxes. That's why it's usually best to take cash instead of property, if you're given the choice. At least you'll be able to set something aside for your taxes and enjoy what's left over.

Of course, you don't *have* to accept a prize or award that's offered to you. If it seems as if the tax problems are going to be too much to handle, simply turn down your winnings. You'll still have the satisfaction of knowing that you won.

Health Insurance Reimbursements

Do you have to pay taxes on a reimbursement check you receive from your health insurance company? Should you report it as income—or can you pocket it tax-free?

If these questions are confusing to you, you're not alone. Health insurance reimbursements can cause sticky problems at tax time.

Example: You're covered by a family health plan. Whenever you or your children visited the doctor during 1980, you paid the bill on the way out. At the end of the year, you gathered these bills together and filed a small claim with your insurance company. You were reimbursed in early 1981.

What do you do with this reimbursement on your 1981 tax return? That depends on whether you itemized your deductions on Schedule A of your 1980 return.

If you *did not* itemize for 1980, your reimbursement check is tax-free.

Even if you *did* itemize, your reimbursement may still be tax-free—*if* you didn't take a medical deduction for that year.

In general, you can deduct medical bills, transportation costs, drug expenses, and so forth that weren't reimbursed or paid for directly by your insurance plan. This deduction is further restricted: You're allowed to take your out-of-pocket medical expenses only to the extent that they exceed 3 percent of your adjusted gross income.

Look at your Schedule A for 1980. It's possible that you listed your interest deductions, charitable contributions, and tax payments but didn't take the medical deduction because of the 3 percent rule. If this is the case, your 1981 reimbursement is tax-free.

Finally, if you *did* itemize in 1980 *and* you deducted the medical bills you were reimbursed for in 1981, then you have to report some or all of this reimbursement as income on line 20 of your 1981 Form 1040.

How much? To find out, recompute your 1980 medical deduction. Determine what your final 1980 tax bill would have been if you hadn't deducted those medical bills you were later reimbursed for. Then compare that amount with your *actual* 1980 tax bill. The difference is the amount you're required to report on your 1981 return.

It sounds complicated, and it can be. However, there are ways to head off this potentially tricky situation. If you file your insurance claims as soon as possible, you may get your reimbursements in time to avoid the carryover from one year to the next. Or, in future years, you may want to forgo claiming medical expenses that you know you'll be reimbursed for later

III.
TAKE ALL OF YOUR
DEDUCTIONS AND CREDITS

Too many people overpay the IRS because they don't take advantage of all the tax breaks available to them. There are literally hundreds of deductions and credits written into the law that most taxpayers don't bother to claim. Sometimes they don't know that these tax breaks exist. But more often they're afraid that claiming deductions and credits will get them audited.

My advice is to take everything the law allows. Why pay more taxes than you have to? If you've kept careful records, you shouldn't have any problem.

Start by considering anything that might even remotely qualify for a tax break. Then carefully check out each item. You'll probably be surprised at what you find.

Whose Deduction Is It?

Each year, too many taxpayers miss large tax deductions simply because they don't take enough time to set up their financial dealings properly.

Example: Your daughter has just graduated from high school and wants to buy her first car. No one will give her the credit unless you guarantee the loan, which you agree to do. You know that this will also give her a start on establishing a credit rating.

As the months go by, she makes the car payments regularly—principle and interest. Then one month she gets sick, misses work, and asks if you'll help out with the debt. You promise to write the check.

But to whom? The bank, or your daughter? The answer to this question determines who will be able to take the interest deduction.

According to the tax rule, you have to satisfy two conditions in order to take this deduction:

1. You must actually make the payment; and

2. You must be legally required to do so.

In this case, if you make the car payment directly to the bank, no one gets the interest deduction. You don't because you're not primarily responsible for paying the loan. Your daughter doesn't because she didn't make the payment.

If you write out the check to your daughter, and she in turn pays her bank, then she gets the interest deduction (*if* she has enough itemized deductions to claim it on her Schedule A).

The only way to qualify for this deduction yourself is to take out the loan in your own name in the first place. Then you make the payments, your daughter sends you a check each month, and you deduct the interest on your return. However, this doesn't help your daughter establish a credit history.

Which is the best way to go? That depends on your own situation.

By the way, the same tax rule applies to other debts as well. This includes personal loans, home mortgages, credit cards, and even medical bills. In each instance, you *can* come up with an arrangement that puts the deductions where they will do the most good—*if* you plan ahead.

Deducting Medical Expenses

Most people are aware that medical expenses are deductible. But a lot of taxpayers aren't sure about whether they can take this deduction and, if so, what kinds of expenses they can claim.

To qualify, your medical expenses must amount to more than 3 percent of your adjusted gross income. In other words, if your adjusted gross income for 1981 was $25,000, you must have paid at least $750 in medical bills out of your own pocket before the next dollar is deductible. If your adjusted gross income was $35,000, you must have paid $1,050 in medical bills before you can take this deduction.

There's one exception to this rule: the cost of your health insurance. You can always deduct one half of your health insurance premiums for the year, up to a maximum of $150. Anything over this limit is deductible as a regular medical expense, subject to the 3 percent requirement.

What kinds of expenses can you deduct? More than you may think. Like the costs of dental and orthodontic work, eyeglasses, contact lenses, and eye exams. Plastic surgery and hair transplants are deductible, even if they're performed only for cosmetic reasons. You can claim what you paid for psychiatric counseling, acupuncture sessions, a legal abortion, and birth control devices. The same goes for hearing aids and batteries. The costs of owning and caring for cats specially trained to aid the deaf and guide dogs for the blind qualify, too. And medically related transportation mileage is deductible at 9¢ a mile.

Caution: The IRS can be very picky about this deduction. One taxpayer whose son had allergies tried to claim a medically prescribed air purifier, a humidifier, a house air conditioner, and air conditioning for his car. The IRS allowed him to deduct these costs—but only to the extent that they exceeded the resulting increase in value of his house and car.

On the other hand, a man with pulmonary disease who replaced a broken compressor on his home air conditioner was permitted to claim the entire cost as a medical expense. The IRS ruled that the compressor was essential to his health.

There are certain things the IRS hardly ever accepts. For example, you probably won't be able to deduct the cost of belonging to a health club, weight-reducing clinic, or stop smoking program. And if your doctor recommends that you buy a treadmill as part of a fitness program to improve an irregular heartbeat, you'll have to bear the expense yourself.

Don't try to deduct personal hygiene items like toothpaste or shaving cream. Diaper service costs and maternity clothes aren't deductible. Neither is marriage counseling.

Under certain circumstances, you may be able to claim part of the cost of a home swimming pool—or even a wig. If you think something may be deductible but you're not sure, check it out with a tax professional.

Two additional points to keep in mind:

1. If you buy an expensive piece of equipment (such as a hospital bed, a wheelchair, or a respirator), you should deduct the full cost for the year of purchase. It doesn't matter if you finance it over a longer period. If you later give the item to charity, you may be able to take another partial deduction at that time.

2. If you pay medical expenses for someone who isn't a tax dependent, you may be able to deduct them anyway.

Example: You pay all of your father's medical bills. He would qualify as your dependent except for the fact that he earns over $1,000 a year. As long as you satisfy the other four requirements for claiming someone as a dependent, you can deduct the medical expenses you pay on his behalf. (See Chapter IV, "Using a Multiple Support Agreement to Claim an Extra Dependent," for an explanation of the dependency requirements.)

Where should you take your medical deduction, if you qualify? On Schedule A of your 1040. You'll have to file the long form.

Of course, you can't claim any expenses that are reimbursed by your insurance company. But if you're only partially reimbursed and your out-of-pocket expenses still exceed 3 percent of your adjusted gross income, then go ahead and write them off.

Deducting Taxes

Too many taxpayers cheat themselves when it comes to deducting the taxes they've paid out all year long. They just don't know about the many kinds of tax payments that qualify for this deduction.

Note: You must file the long form, 1040, and attach Schedule A in order to take this deduction. List the tax payments you're claiming on lines 11 through 16 of Schedule A.

What kinds of taxes are deductible? State and local income taxes, real estate taxes, and general sales taxes. Taken together, they can add up to a sizable tax break.

To determine what to deduct in state and local income taxes, look at your final W-2 for the year. It tells you exactly how much of each was withheld from your paychecks during 1981. If you made any estimated state income tax payments, or paid out extra tax to cover your 1980 bill, don't forget to include these.

Real estate taxes you paid on your home are tax deductible. If your mortgage company makes these payments for you, ask them to give you a grand total for the year. If you make these payments yourself, your cancelled checks can show you how much you paid and serve as proof if the IRS ever challenges you.

Real estate taxes you paid on vacation property are also tax deductible.

If you bought or sold any real estate during the year, you should check your settlement sheets to see what portion of the real estate taxes was paid by you at the settlement and what portion was paid by the other party. You can only deduct the amount you paid.

General sales taxes are deductible, but how you claim them is up to you. You can either use the tables furnished by the IRS (included in their instruction package) or compute this deduction yourself. In general, married couples are better off using the IRS's tables. On the other hand, it's often worth it for single people to figure out exactly how much they paid out in sales taxes. They often come out ahead of the IRS's tables.

If you decide to use the tables, start by determining your adjusted gross income. Add to this all of your tax-free income, like social security or disability benefits, along with the untaxed portion of any long-term capital gains you realized. You'll end up with a higher income level figure, which will allow you to take a bigger sales tax deduction.

If you purchased a new car or truck during the year, don't forget to deduct the general sales tax you paid at the time. (Because this is such a big chunk of money, you can claim it on line 13b in addition to the deduction you're allowed by the IRS's tables.)

A lot of other tax payments simply aren't deductible. For example, you can't claim federal income taxes or social security taxes, both of which are usually withheld from your paychecks. However, federal income taxes aren't a total loss. You can't list them on Schedule A, but you do get to include them on line 55 of your 1040 and directly reduce your tax bill.

What else can't you deduct? State and local gasoline taxes. Taxes you pay on tires, telephone services, and airline tickets. Gift taxes and inheritance taxes. Taxes on tobacco products and alcoholic beverages. Fees for drivers' licenses and auto inspections, dog tags, hunting licenses, and fishing licenses.

Even with these exclusions, you can manage to come up with a hefty deduction if you claim everything you're entitled to.

Deducting Mortgage Interest Payments

The interest you pay on your home mortgage loan may be the single largest deduction you claim on your Schedule A. And, if you're like a lot of taxpayers, you may be claiming less in this area than you're entitled to.

Where do you look when you start figuring this deduction? Probably on the annual statement you receive from your mortgage company. That's supposed to list the amount of interest you paid during the year.

Don't rely on these figures. They're often wrong.

Example: You mail your monthly house payment check

on December 29. Your mortgage company doesn't receive it and credit it to your account until January 4. So when they compile your annual statement, they don't include this payment.

But you should, when it comes to paying your taxes. Call your mortgage company and ask how much of your December payment was interest. They should be able to tell you. Be sure to include this amount in your Schedule A deduction.

Many homeowners receive payment schedules—called amortization schedules—that show how their payments were broken down. If you have one of these, consult it to find out how much you paid in interest every month. Then add these figures together to come up with your deduction.

If you sold a home during the year, look at the settlement sheet you received at the closing. Your mortgage lender charges you interest up to the date of the sale and sometimes even after that time. Some lenders charge interest for an additional two weeks after closing to allow for check clearing and processing, plus an additional penalty for paying off the loan. All of these charges and prepayment penalties are deductible as interest.

If you didn't receive a settlement sheet, ask the settlement attorney or your lender for a copy. The final month's interest may not appear on any of your other records, and you don't want to miss this deduction.

If you bought a new home during the year, you'll receive a mortgage statement at year-end. However, it probably won't include any interest you had to pay at the closing. You're going to have to look on your settlement sheet for items like "interest," "loan processing fees," "loan origination fees," and sometimes even "points." These may all qualify as interest payments—and boost your deduction.

Other Interest Deductions

When you're itemizing your interest deductions on Schedule A of your 1040, don't stop with the interest you paid on your home mortgage. There are many other valuable interest deductions available to you.

If you're like most people today, you probably have several credit cards and charge accounts. Any interest or finance charges you pay on these are tax deductible. So are the interest charges on installment loans.

Most companies or stores you have credit with will total these charges for you and list them on your January statement. If there are some who don't, call them and ask them to send you the totals. Or go back through your monthly bills and add up the figures yourself.

Note: According to the IRS, service charges, loan fees, credit investigation fees, and annual membership fees paid to charge card companies are not deductible. There are two exceptions to this rule: If you pay a one-time charge for a cash advance you get with a bank-style credit card, you can deduct this as an interest payment. And if you have a credit card and use it only for business, you can deduct the membership fee as a business expense.

If you paid interest last year on past due federal or state income taxes, claim it as an itemized deduction. Just make sure that what you paid was in fact interest and not an underpayment penalty (which isn't deductible).

The interest you pay on a personal or secured loan can also be written off. If you took out a loan from a financial institution, they'll send you a statement at year-end reporting your total interest payments. It won't hurt to doublecheck their figures, though. Even bankers make mistakes.

What if you borrow money from a friend or a relative? The law allows you to deduct any interest you pay to him or her during the year—the same as if you were dealing with a bank.

If you take out a loan against your life insurance policy, the interest you pay on that is deductible, too (as long as you don't take out this kind of loan frequently).

Even interest you pay to your stockbroker can be claimed on your Schedule A. However, things get a little tricky when you start linking interest and investments. For example, if you borrow money and use it to buy tax-exempt securities such as an All Savers Certificate or a municipal bond, you can't deduct the interest you pay on the loan.

Keep track of your interest and finance charges throughout

the year. They can add up to a sizable amount by the end of December—and a nice tax break for you.

Deducting Charitable Contributions

Go ahead and deduct all of the charitable contributions you made during the past year. Generally speaking, the IRS won't question this deduction simply because auditors have found that most people are relatively honest about reporting only what they have actually given away.

Add up all of your receipts and cancelled checks showing what you've donated to your local church, school, and other favorite causes. Then list the total on line 21a of your Schedule A, "Cash contributions for which you have receipts or cancelled checks."

Caution: Don't make estimates here. This is one area in which the IRS can become suspicious of round numbers. A deduction of $1,000 could be questioned, while one of $945 might not cause anyone to think twice. However, never let this intimidate you. Claim exactly—and only—what you have contributed to recognized charitable groups and organizations.

What if you don't have cancelled checks and receipts to back up all of your donations? Go to line 21b. Here's where you can deduct your at-the-door and other out-of-pocket cash donations. Like money you dropped into a collection plate, or transportation costs you incurred on behalf of a charity. How much did you give last Easter—$10, $20, or even more? You're allowed to deduct this amount even if you don't have a receipt.

Not all contributions to tax-exempt organizations are deductible. Anything you give to a recognized church, synagogue, school, or nonprofit hospital can be claimed, but a donation to a local homeowners association, social club, or fraternity can't. If you're not sure whether a contribution to a particular group qualifies for tax purposes, call the group and ask. If they can't tell you, call the IRS. They have a special book—Publication 78—that lists all of the tax-exempt organizations to which contributions are deductible.

[37]

There are three questions taxpayers commonly have on this topic:

1. "How much can I deduct of a donation for a benefit performance or fund-raising event?"

Example: You pay $20 for a special showing of a movie to benefit a local charity. But you can only deduct the amount that exceeds the real value of the ticket. In other words, if a movie in your area costs $4, then you can deduct $16.

Even if your ticket or receipt states that the entire amount you paid represents a contribution, you still have to subtract the regular admission price. That's true whether or not you attend the event.

2. "What about raffle tickets?"

Whatever you pay to participate in a raffle, bingo game, or drawing is usually not deductible even if the money benefits a recognized charity. In the eyes of the IRS, it's too much like gambling. However, there can be exceptions to this rule.

My advice is: If you want to make a donation to a charitable organization, do it with a check instead of a raffle ticket.

3. "If someone makes a charitable contribution in my name, who gets the deduction?"

The person who made the contribution does.

Example: Your daughter donates money to a charity in your honor. She takes the deduction. Of course, she has to be able to itemize on Schedule A.

How to Deduct Noncash Donations to Charity

It's easy to deduct cash contributions to charity, but claiming donations of property is another matter. Too many taxpayers shortchange themselves in this area.

You can claim this deduction on line 22 of your Schedule A. But how much of a deduction should you take?

The tax law lets you deduct the *fair market value* of any property you give to a tax-qualified organization (in other words, an organization to which contributions are deductible). It's up to you to decide what the fair market value is, though. And here's where things can get complicated.

Example: During your spring cleaning, you went through

your attic and garage and pulled out all the stuff you haven't used for years. You took some books to your local library, gave some used clothing to your church, and hauled the old furniture that was just taking up space to your community shelter. You wisely kept receipts showing the dates of your donations.

How can you determine their fair market value? Use this rule of thumb: Estimate what a willing buyer would have paid a willing seller for the property in question.

My advice is to *be reasonable* about the values you place on small pieces of property. For each gift worth $200 or less, you can claim your deduction without having to attach an explanatory note to your return.

The IRS starts to take notice of your charity if you claim gifts of more expensive property. For that reason, you should attach a separate statement to your return for any donation you make that's worth over $200. This statement should include the following information:

- A complete description of the gift and the condition it was in when you donated it. (A photograph can be helpful.)
- The name and address of the organization you gave it to.
- The date of your donation.
- How and when you acquired the item.
- The terms of the donation. (Did you place any restrictions on how the charity could use it?)
- The amount you're claiming as a deduction.

Recommendation: If a piece of property is particularly valuable, take the time (and spend the money) to have it appraised. Then attach the appraisal report to your return along with your statement. By the way, you can take the appraisal fee as a miscellaneous itemized deduction.

Not All Charitable Contributions Are Immediately Deductible

Most charitable contributions are fairly simple to deduct. You just claim the amount of money and/or the value of any property you contributed during a given year on that year's tax return.

It's when you want to make a very *large* donation that a serious tax situation may develop.

Let's say that you decide to give something of great value to your church, a local hospital, the college you graduated from, or some other qualifying organization. Like a painting you recently inherited. Some farm land. An antique car. A stamp or coin collection you've had for years. Heirloom furniture. Rare books. Maybe even your home.

How does this affect your taxes?

To begin with, the tax law limits your charitable deduction to a maximum of 50 percent of your adjusted gross income for the year. This means that you may *not* be able to deduct the entire value of your donation—at least, not all at once.

Example: You have a piece of real estate that's worth $65,000. You own it free and clear, and you give it to your church, no strings attached.

At tax time, you figure your adjusted gross income (line 31 on your 1040) and come up with $30,000. Your charitable deduction, in turn, is limited to a maximum of $15,000.

If you made no other charitable donations during the year, this entire amount can come out of the $65,000 piece of property you gave to your church.

But let's say that you gave away another $500 in donations. You can now deduct only $14,500 of your gift to your church.

You must wait until next year to deduct more of your large donation. (Again, the amount of your deduction will depend on your adjusted gross income.) If necessary, you can take up to five years to deduct the entire $65,000 value of your gift.

Caution: Not all contributions qualify for the same deduction rate. Some are limited to a maximum of 20 percent of your adjusted gross income per year. Before you make a donation to a particular group or organization, check with its treasurer to see which rate applies. Or call the IRS. They have a special book—Publication 78—that lists all of the tax-exempt organizations to which contributions are deductible.

Your Time Isn't Worth a Tax Deduction

Every year, people get upset about one area of the tax law or another because it seems illogical or unfair. Like the marriage penalty tax. Or the tax on some unemployment benefits paid to laid-off workers. Or the fact that if you sell your personal residence at a gain, you have to report all of it, but if you sell at a loss you can't take a deduction.

Don't fall into the trap of thinking that taxes should be fair. They aren't. In general, you and the IRS have very different goals. You want to keep as much of your hard-earned money as you can, and the IRS wants to take as much of it as they can get. So there are bound to be points on which you disagree.

One that doesn't make a lot of sense concerns charity work. In short, any time and effort you spend as a volunteer is usually worth nothing as far as deductions go. If you direct a local scout troop, spend a Saturday cleaning up your church's grounds, or coach a little league team, you deserve a pat on the back, but you won't get a tax deduction.

Let's say you donate your valuable, much-in-demand blood to a hospital or the Red Cross. Or you work all night for a telethon. Or you're a highly trained, highly paid professional who spends one day a week at a free clinic. Good for you; too bad for your taxes.

Here's one piece of cheery news: Your out-of-pocket expenses *are* tax deductible.

Example: You travel halfway across the country to attend your favorite charity's annual convention. You're away from home for five days. Your hotel room, meals, and transportation charges are tax deductible. But even though you had to take a week of vacation time—something that's easily valued—you don't get a tax deduction for that. Sorry.

Again, taxes aren't fair. And they probably never will be. Because that's the case, you shouldn't feel bad if you take advantage of the tax loopholes allowed by law. There's absolutely nothing wrong with trying to reduce your tax bill to its lowest legal limit.

[41]

Deducting Casualty and Theft Losses

If your home has ever been burglarized, or your property has ever been damaged by a severe storm, or your wallet or purse has ever been lifted, then you know what a heartache a casualty or theft loss can be. And you probably also know that it can complicate your taxes.

According to the tax law, you're allowed to claim the amount of a casualty or theft loss, less your insurance reimbursement (if any), on Schedule A. If you suffer a business loss, you can deduct your out-of-pocket expenses in full. If your loss is personal, you have to shoulder the first $100 yourself. To claim this deduction, you should also fill out Form 4864, Casualties and Thefts, and attach it to your 1040.

That sounds simple enough, but it's only the tip of the iceberg. The IRS can be very picky when it comes to deciding what does and doesn't qualify as a tax deductible casualty. And here's where things can get messy for you.

For example, the law doesn't take into account the sentimental value of a stolen or damaged object. Just because something is priceless to you doesn't mean that the IRS will feel the same way about it.

Often this tax break won't cover the cost of replacing a specific object. And because of the $100 rule on personal losses, it may not put any money in your pocket at all.

Example: You bought some lawn furniture for $100 four years ago. Recently a tree branch fell on it and smashed it. Unfortunately, your insurance won't cover the damage.

Even though it would cost more that $250 to buy that same furniture today, your loss is worth about $40 as far as the IRS is concerned. That's what a used furniture store might have given you for your set before it was damaged.

Can you go ahead and deduct the $40? The answer is no. That amount is less than the $100 you're supposed to absorb yourself for a personal casualty loss.

There are some losses that are almost always deductible. If the windows in your house are broken by a sonic boom, you can claim these damages. If you have to repair your roof after a heavy snowstorm, you can deduct the costs.

However, others are almost never deductible. What if your home is invaded by termites or your clothes are ruined by moths? Sorry, no deduction. The same goes for dry rot.

What if your house is severely damaged by a tornado and you have to move your family to a motel for a while? The unreimbursed storm damage is deductible, but your temporary living costs aren't. Neither is any decline in the market value of your property caused by the storm.

If you lose your wallet or leave your camera in the woods, the IRS won't give you a tax break for your carelessness.

At times, the law regarding casualty losses seems a little strange. For example, if your hot water heater explodes and destroys rugs, drapes, and furniture, you can deduct these losses—but not the damage to the heater itself.

If you do claim a casualty or theft loss on your tax return, you may have to prove that you're entitled to it. My advice is to keep an up-to-date list of your valuables in a safety deposit box. Include a description of each item, its purchase price (along with a copy of the receipt, if possible), and about how much you'd get for it if you sold it today. Have valuables appraised. Then you'll at least have some idea of what to claim if and when the time comes.

Cover your bases in other ways, too. If your house is burglarized, call in the police and get it on record. Notify your insurance company if something you own is stolen or damaged. Take photographs.

Other than that, about all you can do is to deduct what you're entitled to and let the IRS decide if your claim is valid.

One final point: The tax law says that you're supposed to deduct a casualty loss for the tax year when it occurred. But if you're filing an insurance claim, you're supposed to hold off until you find out how much your insurance company is going to pay.

When to File an Insurance Claim— and When to Deduct a Casualty Loss

If you suffered a casualty loss sometime during 1981— if your home was burglarized, or you were involved in an automobile accident, or you experienced any one of a hundred different losses—then you may qualify for a tax deduction on this year's return.

Under the tax law, you're allowed to deduct any damage to your automobile of over $100. You can also deduct any loss due to vandalism or theft over that amount that hasn't been or won't be covered by your insurance. The IRS says that if you are insured you must file a claim (and be refused) in order to take this deduction. (Or, if you're partially reimbursed, you can only deduct the unreimbursed amount.)

But let's face it—there are times when it's best *not* to file an insurance claim. For example: Your vacation home is burglarized. You've already filed three other claims this year, and you're afraid that another will result in your policy being cancelled. Or: You run your boat onto the rocks, and your agent tells you that all of your other policies will be revoked if you make one more claim. Or: Your 16-year-old son has a minor fender-bender with the family car. Filing a claim on the damage will double or even triple your rates.

In cases like these, you should definitely notify your insurance company. It may be wiser in the long run, though, to skip filing a claim and absorb the costs yourself rather than risk higher rates or cancellation.

If that's what you decide to do, you can deduct your loss on Schedule A of your tax return. And you can do this in spite of the IRS's position. That's because the Tax Court disagrees with the IRS on this issue.

According to the judges, people who suffer casualty losses but are unwilling to file claims (for fear of cancellation or higher rates) should be treated the same under the tax law as people who carry no insurance at all or are self-insured.

This means that you have two options when it comes to a casualty loss:

1. You can either file a claim with your insurance company; or

2. You can pay for the loss yourself and deduct it.

If you haven't been able to deduct past casualty losses (for which you weren't reimbursed) because of the IRS's position, you should consider filing an amended return on Form 1040X. The IRS might object, but the Tax Court is on your side.

Deducting the Costs of an Office in Your Home

A lot of people are in business for themselves these days. They consult, do freelance writing or graphic designing, sew, weave, make pottery, upholster furniture—all kinds of things. Some are self-employed full-time, while others run sideline businesses in addition to working nine-to-five for someone else.

Many of these fledgling entrepreneurs maintain offices in their homes. Depending on how it's handled, an office in the home can lead to valuable tax deductions.

To qualify, you must satisfy three very strict requirements:

1. You must use that portion of your home *exclusively* as an office; *and*

2. You must use it as an office on a *regular* basis; *and*

3. You must use it as your *principal* place of business.

In other words, a corner of the kitchen doesn't count. Neither does a room you work in once or twice a month. Even if you're self-employed full-time, you can't deduct your study at home if your main office is somewhere else.

Note: If you have a secondary office in your home that you use for meetings with patients, clients, or customers, you may be able to deduct your costs. But you'll have to be able to prove that you use it regularly—and only—for meetings.

In general, your chances of being able to claim these deductions are rather slim if you are an employee. For example, if you're a teacher and you set up your spare bedroom as a place to grade papers, it will be helpful for you but it won't be deductible. The same goes if you're a staff attorney and you study legal briefs in your den every night. Even though you may often need to work at home, you won't get this tax break because your primary office is elsewhere.

There is an exception to this rule: If you have an office in your home for your employer's convenience—not just yours—you can go ahead and take your deductions.

If you do qualify, what kinds of things can you claim? Utility charges, upkeep, depreciation (if you own your home), a portion of your rent (if you don't), your business telephone, air conditioning, office furniture, supplies, a reference library, tools—almost anything you need to keep your home office going. You'll have to figure out how much of your residence is taken up by your office. Once you come up with a percentage, apply it to your monthly utility bills, rent payments, and so on. Claim these costs against your business income.

Where should you take your deductions? If your business isn't incorporated (most businesses operated out of people's homes aren't), fill out Schedule C, Profit or Loss from Business or Profession, and attach it to your 1040. You'll have to file the long form.

Deducting Travel Expenses

If your job keeps you on the move—if you're always hopping a plane to meet with out-of-town clients and associates, or driving to a branch office in another city—then you may have a tax break coming.

Example: Your employer sends you across the country to attend a two-day seminar. You pay for your plane fare, your taxis to and from the airport, a rental car, your hotel, and restaurant meals.

If your company picks up the tab or reimburses you for all of your expenses, you don't get a deduction. If you're only partially reimbursed, you can claim the difference. And if you foot the whole bill yourself, you can deduct every dollar.

Where should you take this deduction? If you're an employee, you'll have to fill out IRS Form 2106, Employee Business Expenses, and attach it to your 1040. If you're self-employed, use Schedule C, Profit or Loss from Business or Profession.

If your travel deduction for the year turns out to be substantial (in relation to the income you report), it may attract the IRS's attention. That's why it's *very* important to keep close track of your expenses.

My advice is to carry a pocket-size business calendar and diary with you at all times. Use it to jot down your itinerary for each business trip, where you stayed, where you ate, the names of the people you met with, and so on. Be sure to ask for—and keep—receipts. Don't forget taxi fare chits.

If you're ever audited, here's what you'll have to be ready and able to show the IRS:

- Documentation to verify every expense you're claiming for business travel. You must have a receipt or a credit card slip for anything over $25, but it helps if you can back up even smaller amounts.
- When you left home and returned from each trip.
- How long you spent on each trip, and if there were any days when you visited friends and relatives on the side.
- Where you stayed.
- The reason for your trip, and the business benefit you expected to gain from it. (If you went out of town to finalize a deal and the deal fell through, you can still deduct your expenses.)

If you're entitled to a big deduction, go ahead and take it. Just be prepared to prove it if you have to.

Note: Some taxpayers combine business and pleasure and still qualify for this deduction. If you meet with a client or a business associate while you're on vacation, you may be able to deduct part of your expenses. Just don't get carried away.

Deducting Entertainment Expenses

It's often easier to conduct business in a social setting than in a stuffy office atmosphere. A lot of deals are closed over dinner or cocktails, at the country club, on the golf course, at the football stadium, or even at the theater.

Regardless of whether you run your own business or are employed by someone else, you may be called upon to entertain business associates and clients. Your entertainment expenses are deductible—as long as you can back them up.

You should know that the IRS has a history of auditing returns that show large entertainment deductions. If you're called in for an audit, the IRS will want you to verify each and every amount you claim. And they'll ask some hard questions.

That's why it's *very* important to keep careful records of

your entertainment expenses. The best way to do this is to carry a pocket-size business calendar and diary with you at all times. Write down in it the particulars of any business entertaining you pay for. And do it after each event, while it's fresh in your mind. Be sure to keep receipts—theater ticket stubs, taxi chits, credit card slips, and so on. The more documentation you have, the better off you'll be.

Here's the kind of information you'll have to give the IRS if they ever challenge your entertainment deduction:

- The date of each outing.
- How much you spent.
- The name and address of each place you went to, along with the type of entertainment provided (a ball game, dinner, a movie, etc.)
- The reason for the outing, and the business benefit you expected to gain from it. (If an evening didn't turn out the way you wanted it to, you can still deduct your expenses.)
  - Each guest's occupation, along with his or her relationship to your company or business.

What if you can't prove a particular item you're claiming? The IRS auditor can turn it down.

Some business-related entertainment expenses are more obviously deductible than others. There's usually no question about the cost of a hospitality suite at a convention, for example, or a luncheon for civic leaders and corporate executives. But a lot of taxpayers don't realize that the money they spend on taking a client to dinner or for cocktails is also deductible—as long as business is discussed somewhere along the line.

And if the outing closely follows a business meeting, you may not have to talk business at all and you'll still be able to take your deduction.

Example: You have a late-afternoon meeting with a client in your office. Afterward, you and your spouse take your client and his or her spouse to dinner. Even though no one breathes a word about the deal you discussed earlier, you can go ahead and claim your expenses when you file your tax return.

Where should you take your entertainment deduction? If you're an employee, fill out IRS Form 2106, Employee Business Expenses, and attach it to your 1040. If you're self-employed, use Schedule C, Profit or Loss from Business or Profession.

Deducting Country Club
and Other Club Dues and Fees

A great many people belong to country clubs. Even more have joined sporting, social, and athletic clubs. With today's concern for good health and physical fitness, club memberships are becoming increasingly common.

If you belong to a club, you may qualify for two excellent tax breaks:

1. You may be able to deduct some or all of your dues, fees, and other expenses associated with your annual membership; and

2. You may be able to deduct all of your out-of-pocket expenses associated with your use of the club's facilities.

Here's the rule: You're allowed to claim a tax deduction for those membership fees and expenses that are directly related to your *business* use of your club. If half of the time you spent there in 1981 was related to business, you can deduct half of your fees and assessments on IRS Form 2106, Employee Business Expenses. If 75 percent of the time you spent there was business related, you can deduct 75 percent of your annual fees.

However, if less than half of the time you spent at the club during the past year was business related, you can't deduct any of your annual fees.

It's easy to determine whether you qualify for this deduction—*if* you kept good records last year. Start by adding up all of the days you spent at your club for any reason, whether business or personal. Then identify those occasions when you took a client for a business conversation, round of golf, or dinner. Finally, figure out the percentage of time you spent at your club on business.

Even if you can't deduct any of your annual fees, you can

still deduct all of your business-related out-of-pocket expenses for food, drink, greens fees, pool passes, saunas, and so on. You must be able to verify the date, the name of the person you entertained, and your business relationship with that person. That's why it's important to keep careful records. One of the simplest ways to do this is to carry a small pocket diary and make detailed daily notes in it.

Example: You belong to an athletic club and used it approximately 50 times during the past year. Only twice did you take a business associate with you for a workout and a swim. Obviously, you can't deduct any of your annual membership dues since you didn't use the club more than 50 percent of the time on business. But you can deduct anything you spent on your guests on these two occasions—as long as you can prove it.

In general, the IRS doesn't like to allow this deduction, and auditors tend to turn it down whenever they get the chance. Don't let that stop you from deducting something you're allowed to take, though. If you use your club for business 100 percent of the time, then go ahead and deduct all of your fees and expenses.

On those occasions when the IRS does deny this deduction, it's usually because people's records are too sketchy. The better your records, the better your chances of keeping this deduction.

Deducting Driving Costs

Don't shortchange yourself when deducting your business driving expenses. If you use your car for business errands or out-of-town trips, take your deduction on IRS Form 2106, Employee Business Expenses. (You'll have to file the long form, 1040, if you want to take advantage of this tax break.)

There are two ways to figure your driving expenses:

1. You can either claim your actual out-of-pocket costs; *or*

2. You can use the IRS's optional standard mileage rate.

Which is best for you? Well, the top rate the IRS now offers is 20¢ a mile, but it costs anywhere from 30¢ to 40¢ a mile just to keep a car on the road today. So obviously it's better to figure your actual expenses, if at all possible. You'll come out ahead.

Add up what you paid during 1981 for gasoline, oil, insurance premiums, registration fees, tires, maintenance, and repairs. Don't forget depreciation, especially if your car is newer or expensive.

Note: If you use your car for both business and personal transportation, you can only deduct a portion of these costs. Determine approximately how much of your driving was strictly business-related and deduct this percentage.

You may decide that you'd rather use the IRS's optional standard mileage rate. If this is the case, you can generally deduct 20¢ a mile for the first 15,000 business miles you drove and 11¢ for each additional mile.

Regardless of which method you choose, the IRS allows you to add to your deduction anything you spent on business-related parking fees and highway tolls. (Sorry, but parking fines and other tickets aren't deductible.)

What will you have to prove if you're ever audited? That depends on how you figured your deduction. If you used the actual expense method, you'll need your receipts and/or cancelled checks. If you used the optional mileage rates method, you'll have to verify the number of miles you drove on business.

Proving your mileage may not be easy, especially if you didn't keep close track of your business driving during 1981. It will help if you have receipts listing your odometer reading at particular times.

If you live in a state or county that requires annual or semi-annual vehicle inspections, your mileage may have been recorded on the inspection receipt. You may also find it on repair bills.

What if you absolutely can't come up with a single receipt or document to prove your mileage for the year? Go out to your car *now* and write down the current odometer reading. This will at least give you some sort of reference point if you're ever called in for an audit.

By the way, the IRS normally doesn't allow deductions for personal driving expenses. In other words, you can't write off the costs of driving to and from work each day or going to the grocery store. However, they will let you deduct 9¢ a mile for driving associated with a job-related move (Form 3903), medical transportation (Schedule A, line 6c), and driving for charity (Schedule A under "contributions"). Although it's probably easier to use the 9¢ optional mileage rate, you might be better off if you figure your actual expenses.

Deducting Job Hunting Expenses

Tens of thousands of taxpayers are missing a legitimate tax break: what they spend while looking for a new job. Your expenses may be substantial, or they may only amount to $100, but every little bit helps when you're trying to reduce your overall tax bill. So if you bought lunch for someone who could become your new employer, made long-distance telephone calls, or incurred any other out-of-pocket costs associated with hunting for a new job, you can take a tax deduction—in full.

You can claim your expenses for travel, transportation, meals, and lodging on IRS Form 2106, Employee Business Expenses. In other words, you don't have to itemize your other deductions (such as medical, interest, charity, etc.) on Schedule A to claim these job hunting expenses.

But if you want to deduct related costs—like the money you spend having your resume typed and printed, the postage you use to mail out information about yourself, etc.—you must use Schedule A. Add up all of your expenses. If the total is relatively small—under a couple hundred dollars—list it beneath the "miscellaneous" heading and write "job hunting expenses" beside it. If the total exceeds $200, attach a separate sheet itemizing these expenses to your Schedule A. You don't have to write a note explaining this deduction.

Here are a few points to keep in mind:

1. To be entitled to deduct your job seeking expenses, you must be looking for a new job *in the same trade or business* as your current position. If you're looking in a new field, none of your expenses are deductible.

Recommendation: If you find that this restriction is going to knock out your job hunting deduction, try to reclassify your present job. When you list your occupation on the front of your tax return, be as general as possible. For example, call yourself a manager, administrator, or assistant rather than using your specific title.

2. You don't have to be vigorously pursuing a new job in order to deduct related expenses. If you go out of town on a vacation, for example, an interview with a firm that's similar to the one you already work for can lead to a valuable deduction. Naturally, you'll want to thoroughly document this interview.

3. Your expenses are tax deductible whether or not you actually get a new job.

4. Employment agency fees are deductible as long as you're looking in the field you're already in.

5. If a prospective employer from another city asks you to come in for an interview and pays you an allowance or reimburses you for your travel expenses, this money is tax-free to you. But if the amount you receive turns out to be more than your actual expenses (which is unlikely), you must pay taxes on the excess.

6. If you're unemployed, you can still deduct job hunting expenses if the job you're looking for is related to the last one you had. But if you've gone a long time between jobs, the IRS will probably not allow this deduction.

7. If you're looking for your first job, none of your job hunting expenses are deductible. Sorry, but that's the law.

Deducting Work Clothes and Other Special Clothing

Clothing can be expensive, especially if your job requires you to dress well and keep up with current fashion trends. Unfortunately, the IRS doesn't usually let you deduct the costs of buying and maintaining the clothes you wear at work.

However, there are exceptions to this rule. You may be

able to deduct the costs of buying, repairing, and cleaning your work clothes *if* they satisfy two exacting conditions:

1. They must be required by your employer and essential to your occupation; *and*

2. They must not be suitable for everyday use.

Example: The manager of an exclusive (and expensive) boutique wanted to deduct the cost of her designer clothes, claiming that her employer required her to wear them at the shop. She wouldn't normally have bought these clothes for herself—they didn't fit her usual life-style—and she only wore them at work. Nevertheless, the IRS and the court turned down her deduction. Why? Because some members of society *do* wear designer clothes on the street. In other words, the woman's work clothing was judged suitable for everyday use.

The question of what is deductible and what isn't applies mainly to uniforms. If you're a professional ball player, fire fighter, police officer, letter carrier, jockey, or nurse, go ahead and take this deduction. If you're a transportation employee—like a pilot or a flight attendant—you can deduct the cost of your uniforms as long as you wear them only at work. One flight attendant tried to deduct her shoes, purses, and cosmetics; the IRS said no because these items could also be used outside of her job.

If you're a musician or an entertainer, you can deduct the cost of the uniforms, costumes, other clothing, and accessories you wear exclusively for performing.

If you use protective clothing on the job, its cost is generally tax deductible. This includes items like safety shoes, hard hats, work gloves, oil clothes, and rubber boots. But coveralls and gear that do nothing but protect your other clothing aren't tax deductible.

If you're on full-time active duty in the armed forces, you can't deduct the costs of purchasing or maintaining your uniforms. In the eyes of the IRS, your uniforms take the place of civilian clothes. You can claim the costs of any insignia, braids, bars, swords, and epaulets you wear, though, since they aren't considered part of normal everyday clothing.

If you're in the reserves, you can deduct your uniform costs. Of course, you must reduce this deduction by the allowance the government pays you for this purpose.

Where should you take this deduction? On Schedule A of your Form 1040. Add up the costs of your work clothing and list the total on line 31.

Home Security Systems: Are They Deductible?

With the crime rate being what it is today, more and more people are installing security devices in their homes. These range from fancy grillwork that go over windows and doors to sirens, automatic lighting, and sophisticated "silent alarms" that communicate directly with local law-enforcement offices.

Are these deductible, or aren't they? It all depends on what you're trying to protect.

Example: You own some valuables—a painting, some jewelry, televisions, stereos, cameras, silverware. You live in a big city, and you're afraid of being burglarized. So you purchase an expensive home security system.

According to the IRS, the cost of *this* system is *not* deductible. Why? Because you bought it to protect your *personal* valuables.

However, they *may* let you deduct at least part of your system's cost *if* you can show in the event of an audit that you bought it to protect items that you are holding *primarily as investments*. Like a stamp collection, an oriental rug, or antique furniture.

In other words, the cost of protecting investments is considered deductible while the cost of safeguarding your home, personal property, and family isn't. As strange as it may seem, that's the law.

Where should you take this deduction, if your system qualifies as an investment expense? On Schedule A under "miscellaneous deductions." You'll have to file the long form, 1040.

How much of a deduction should you take? That's not an easy question to answer. I wish I could give you a formula to use when figuring out what percentage of your system to claim, but there isn't one.

My advice is to go ahead and deduct all of your costs, plus installation, if you buy a home security system to protect your investments. If you purchase one for safety's sake, you can't deduct any of your costs.

If you're audited, be prepared to tell the IRS about your investments—what they consist of, where you keep them, and why you think it's necessary to protect them. It will help if you have a history of buying and selling certain types of investment items, such as artwork and antiques.

Deducting Educational Expenses

The importance of a good education increases every day. So do the costs. That's why you should let the IRS pick up part of the tab, if possible. How? By deducting some or all of your educational expenses.

If you're employed and you're required to take certain courses to maintain your present job, salary, or title, you can take advantage of this tax break. If you must constantly update your education to keep your certification in a career such as teaching, medicine, law, or accounting, these expenses are deductible.

You may even be able to deduct the costs of courses that aren't required. If they will help you to keep up or improve the skills you use in your current job, the IRS will usually let you write them off.

Example: You're a flight engineer, and your employer wants you to obtain a commercial pilot's license. So you sign up for training courses. Since you're improving your job skills, and your employer has asked you to take these courses, you can deduct whatever they cost you.

What educational expenses are deductible? Tuition, books, and supplies. Lab fees and other related fees. Correspondence courses, tutoring, and research assistance may qualify.

Don't forget about transportation costs. If you go to school directly from your office, you can deduct the mileage from your job to your class and from your class to your home. If you go home before heading off to class, you can deduct the mileage to and from school. The IRS allows you to claim 20¢ a mile for driving associated with your education.

Add your expenses together and list the total under "miscellaneous deductions" on Schedule A. (You'll have to file the long form, 1040.) Identify this deduction as "educational expenses."

The IRS also needs to know where you go to school and what courses you take. So you should either fill out and file Form 2106, Employee Business Expenses (Part III), or write an explanatory note and attach it to your return.

Of course, if your employer reimburses you for the costs of your education, you can't claim this deduction. If you're only partially reimbursed, go ahead and deduct your net out-of-pocket expenses.

What if you take courses that may lead to a new trade or business? Sorry, but these aren't deductible. To qualify for the educational expenses tax break, any courses you take must be related to your present job.

What if you have to take courses to meet the minimal standards of a position you've applied for or eventually want to hold? These aren't deductible either. If you must finish your nursing degree before the local hospital will hire you, you'll have to bear these expenses yourself.

Deducting Tax Advice

Tax advice is expensive, to say the least. It's a shame that taxes are as complicated as they are—and that you have to study, plan, and consult with experts in order to reduce your tax bill to its lowest legal limit.

I do have one piece of good news, though: Tax advice is deductible. If you itemize your deductions this year, you can claim any fees you paid to your financial advisor and/or tax preparer for tax work done in 1981. Add them together and claim the total as a miscellaneous itemized deduction on line 30b of your Schedule A.

Expenses you pay to defend your return during an IRS audit are also tax deductible. So is the cost of any book or magazine you buy to help you figure your taxes.

In other words, the purchase price of this book is tax deductible. Just be sure to keep your receipt.

The Political Contributions Credit

How would you like to cut your tax bill by $50 or $100? It's easy if you're the least bit politically active. All you have to do is claim a tax credit for the political contributions you made during the year.

This tax break is one of the easiest to claim, and it's basically risk-free as far as triggering an IRS audit is concerned. It's there for the taking, regardless of whether you itemize your tax credits on the long form, 1040, or simply file the short form, 1040A.

Here's the rule on tax credits for political contributions: You can take a tax credit for one-half of the political contributions you made during the year. If you're filing singly, this credit can't exceed $50. In other words, if you made political contributions totaling $60 in 1981, you can claim half ($30); if your contributions totaled $100, you can claim half ($50); if they totaled $500, you can still only claim $50.

A married couple filing jointly can take a tax credit for one-half of their contributions, up to a maximum credit of $100.

Of course, you should keep written receipts to back up your claim. Your cancelled check is usually good enough proof.

There are some restrictions you should be aware of. Namely, your contribution must have been made to a recognized or qualified political candidate or campaign committee, or to the national, state, or local committee of a national political party.

I have bad news for volunteers. All of your time and effort isn't worth a tax credit on your return. In order to claim this credit, you must have made an actual out-of-pocket cash contribution.

The Earned Income Credit

One of the best tax breaks around for lower income families is the so-called "earned income tax credit." If you qualify, you can claim this credit on either the short form, 1040A (line 13c), or the long form, 1040 (line 57).

What makes you eligible for this credit? To begin with, your 1981 income must have been under $10,000. If it was, *and* you worked during the year (that is, you took in salary, tips, or self-employment earnings), *and* you have a dependent child, then you qualify.

It's relatively easy to figure out the amount of your earned income tax credit. Use the worksheet that the IRS includes in your tax package. Just follow all of the steps and you shouldn't have any trouble. (Don't send your worksheet along with your return; the IRS won't need it. Store it in a safe place along with your other tax records.)

If you're married, by the way, then you and your spouse must file jointly. You can't each file separately and claim this credit.

What if the credit reduces your taxes to below zero? That's terrific! The IRS will refund any excess to you.

If you've already filed your 1981 return without claiming the earned income tax credit, and you're entitled to it, don't worry. You won't have to file an amended return in order to get your money. The IRS is on the lookout for taxpayers who don't know about this credit. They'll compute it for you and send you a check.

The Residential Energy Credit

We're all becoming more energy conscious these days. Most of us are doing our best to cut down on our energy consumption. Those of us who make our homes more efficient get a tax break: the residential energy tax credit.

This credit sounds good, and it is—if you know how it works.

There are actually *two* different energy credits you can claim: one for energy conservation items, and one for renewable energy source items.

Here's what the law says about energy conservation items:

You can take a tax credit amounting to 15 percent of the

first $2,000 you spend on insulation, storm windows and doors, caulking, and weatherstripping. You can also claim the costs of buying and installing an automatic setback thermostat, an ignition system that replaces a gas pilot light, and a modified fuel system. Just keep in mind the 15 percent rule. This limits your *maximum* credit to $300.

This credit is subject to three other restrictions:

1. You must use the energy conservation items in your personal residence. Vacation homes don't count.

2. The most you can put into any one home for residential energy tax credit purposes is $2,000. In other words, if you spent $1,500 on storm doors and windows last year, that leaves you with only $500 to spend in later years that will qualify for this credit.

3. Your principal residence must have been substantially completed before April 20, 1977. If it was built after that, you can't take this credit.

Note: If you move, and your new home was built before the April 20, 1977 deadline, you can start all over again by spending $2,000 on energy conservation items and taking the full $300 credit.

The second energy credit—the one that has to do with renewable energy source items—is a bit less restricted. It applies to both older and newer homes. When claiming this credit, you don't have to worry about when your house was built.

What are renewable energy source items? Anything that uses sun, wind, or geothermal energy. This includes solar collectors and panels and heat exchangers.

If you install any of these in your home, you can take a tax credit amounting to 40 percent of the first $10,000 you spend. This works out to a maximum credit of $4,000. Again, this is the most you can ever claim for improvements made to any one home.

Caution: Some energy saving items don't qualify for either tax credit, no matter how much warmer they make your home. Awnings, shades, carpeting, heat pumps, and fluorescent lights aren't deductible.

Good news for renters: You don't have to own your home in order to qualify for this tax break. If you pay for energy improvements made to your rented apartment or house, you get to take the credit.

Where should you claim this credit? On IRS Form 5695, Residential Energy Credit. And you'll have to file the long form, 1040.

How to Retrieve Overpaid Social Security Taxes

Did you hold down more than one job in 1981 or switch to a higher-paying position? If you did, *and* if you earned over $29,700, you may have had too much in social security taxes (FICA) withheld from your paychecks. And you may qualify for a nice little tax break as a result.

Why $29,700? Because that was the 1981 social security earnings limit.

Example: You earned $18,000 during the first nine months of 1981. You then moved on to a better job. During the last three months of the year, you earned another $8,000 in salary plus a $6,000 bonus, bringing your annual wages to a grand total of $32,000.

Your first employer took out social security taxes on the full $18,000 paid to you. Your second employer withheld social security on the $14,000 you earned on your new job. In other words, your payroll taxes were overpaid.

By how much? Subtract the 1981 social security earnings limit ($29,700) from your earnings ($32,000). The $2,300 difference is free from social security taxes. Since the tax rate for 1981 was 6.65 percent, your overpayment came to $152.95.

Claim this amount on line 59 of your Form 1040. It's considered a tax payment, which means money in your pocket.

Note: If you had only one employer during the year, you should still check your W-2, Annual Wage Statement, if your salary was over $29,700. Make sure that your employer didn't mistakenly continue to withhold social security taxes from your paychecks once your earnings exceeded the limit. As an employee, you should not have paid more than $1,975.05 in social security taxes for 1981.

[61]

If your employer did withhold too much in social security taxes, you're not allowed to take a credit on your tax return for the overpayment. But you can ask for—and get—a refund of the excess directly from the company.

Deducting Moving Expenses

A job-related move can be costly. Even the IRS recognizes this. They'll let you take your moving expenses as a deduction on your tax return—*if* you satisfy two requirements:

1. Your new work place must be at least 35 miles farther from your former home than your old work place was.

Here's what this means: Figure out how far it is from your new work site to your former home. Then figure out how far it is from your old work site to your former home. Take the difference between the two. If it's at least 35 miles, you're okay.

If you're unemployed, get a job offer, and move, your place of business must be at least 35 miles from your old home.

2. You must work for at least 39 out of the first 52 weeks following your move. If you're self-employed, you must work for at least 78 weeks out of the next two years.

The second requirement—the so-called "work rule"—worries a lot of people.

Example: You moved in 1981 to take a better paying job. But you won't have worked for 39 weeks until sometime in 1982. When should you take your moving expenses deduction? On your 1981 tax return. It's assumed that you *will* work the full 39 weeks. If you don't, you'll have to make an adjustment on your 1982 return or file an amended return on Form 1040X for 1981.

You must file the long form, 1040, in order to claim this deduction. However, you don't have to itemize on Schedule A. Simply fill out Form 3903, Moving Expense Adjustments, and attach it to your return.

You can deduct the on-the-road travel expenses incurred during your job-related move in one of two ways. Either keep track of your actual expenses for gas, oil, etc. and deduct

[62]

the total, *or* record your mileage and deduct the 9¢ per mile rate allowed by the IRS. Whatever method you choose, be sure to add in any parking fees and highway tolls.

The costs of moving your possessions are also deductible. These include any payments you make to moving companies and/or fees for rental trailers, pads, packing, crating, shipping, and insurance.

In addition, you can deduct up to $3,000 in related expenses. Did your move mean that you had to break a lease? These costs are deductible. Did you pay closing costs when you bought a new home or sold your old one? These are deductible, too.

You may even be able to claim some of the costs of trips you made to your new location before your move, and up to 30 days' worth of temporary living expenses.

Anyone who moved during 1981 should at least consider this tax break. You may be surprised to discover that you qualify for it.

Example: You're retiring and you want to relocate. You're considering setting up a small business of your own once you've moved. If you do, and if you plan to work for 78 weeks out of the next two years, you can claim your moving expenses.

Example: You're about to graduate from college when a recruiter offers you a job with her firm in another state. You accept the offer.

Because you're just starting, your new employer won't pay your moving costs, so you agree to pay them yourself. You take a quick trip to see what the area is like. Later you spend two weeks living in a motel before you find an apartment.

What can you deduct? The costs of your first visit, the costs of your move, and the costs of staying in the motel while you were apartment hunting.

Individual Retirement Accounts (IRAs)—1981

It's not too late to think about an Individual Retirement Account for 1981. According to the law, you still have time to open an IRA or fund your pre-existing plan from 1981 or earlier. In fact, you have until April 15, 1982 (the day your 1981 tax return is due) to open and/or fund your 1981 IRA. And if you ask the IRS for an automatic 60-day extension of time to file your return, you can handle your 1981 IRA business as late as June 14.

A 1981 IRA could be a valuable tax-saving tool for you. That's because your IRA contribution is deductible—in full. (You must file the long form in order to take this deduction.) In addition, any interest it earns is tax deferred.

However, you must meet strict eligibility requirements if you want to open or pay into an IRA for 1981. Specifically: You must *not* have been employed during that calendar year by a company offering a tax-qualified retirement plan. It doesn't matter whether or not you participated in the plan. Even if you spent only *one day* as an employee of a firm with a pension plan of its own, you forfeited your right to open an IRA for 1981. You also forfeited your right to make a 1981 contribution to a pre-existing IRA.

What if you properly opened an IRA in 1980, but then went to work in 1981 for a firm with a pension plan? Although you can't put any money into your IRA for 1981, you should maintain it. Don't try to cash it in, or you'll have to pay a premature withdrawal penalty. Any interest it earned during 1981 will continue to be tax deferred, since the IRS doesn't treat accumulated interest in the same way as a contribution to your plan.

If you are eligible to open an IRA for 1981, how much can you put into it? As a general rule, the law limits your contribution to a maximum of $1,500 or 15 percent of your salary for that year, whichever is smaller. Married couples with only one wage earner may set up what are termed "spousal IRAs"— one for each partner—and contribute up to $1,750 divided equally between the two accounts. The 15 percent limit applies here, too.

If you do want to open an IRA for 1981 or make a contribution to a pre-existing IRA, be sure to note right on your check the year the money is intended for. In other words, carefully document what you're doing now in case you're called in for an audit later. You'll also want to have this proof on hand if you decide to make another contribution to your IRA for 1982.

Caution: Because of the 1981 Economic Recovery Tax Act, you have to keep two sets of rules in mind when thinking about IRAs—one for 1981, and another for 1982. (See Chapter I for the 1982 rules.) A simple, innocent mixup between the two years could cost you money.

IV.

SPECIAL CASES

Most tax situations are fairly straightforward. However, there are some that don't fit into nice, neat categories within the tax law.

Special cases require special planning. If your personal circumstances are unusual, or if you have a unique tax problem, you'll need to consider your options very carefully. Your decision can make the difference between a costly tax trap and a valuable tax break.

Income Averaging

Income averaging is without a doubt one of the best tax breaks on the books. Unfortunately, too many people either don't know about it or don't know how it works.

Income averaging was originally intended to help taxpayers with fluctuating incomes—people like writers and consultants. The idea behind it was to "spread" their incomes out over a number of years, at least for tax purposes, so they wouldn't be saddled with exceptionally high tax bills at any given time. But today almost anyone who receives bonuses, raises, and cost-of-living adjustments may qualify for income averaging.

If you've never even considered income averaging, you should. It can't possibly hurt you. If you find that it won't lower your taxes this year, it may the next.

Go through your records and pull out copies of your tax returns for the past four years. Write down your taxable income figure for each of these years. Then get a copy of Schedule G, Income Averaging, for 1981 and follow the instructions on it.

If the figure you end up with on line 14 is $3,000 or less, stop. Income averaging *won't* help you this year. File the worksheet with your tax records for 1982 so you can try again next year.

But if the figure on line 14 is more than $3,000, go ahead and finish Schedule G. You'll come up with a tax liability amount.

Now prepare your 1040 as usual. (You can't income average if you use the short form, 1040A.) Compare the tax figure on line 35 with the one shown on your completed Schedule G. The lower number is the one that goes on your final tax return. It's that simple.

Be sure to check the box marked "Schedule G" on line 35 of your 1040. And don't forget to attach your Schedule G to your return before you mail it.

Here's a quick and easy technique you can use to determine whether income averaging might lower your taxes this year: Add together your taxable income figures for 1977–80, multiply the total by 30 percent, and add $3,000. If the resulting number is lower than your 1981 taxable income, you can probably income average to your benefit.

You can income average every year, as long as you qualify. You'll need four years' worth of tax returns in order to start, but you won't have to wait four more years before doing it again.

Note: Income averaging only works for years when your income is up. For years when it's down, you won't be able to use it. But you should always fill out a Schedule G, just in case, and keep it on hand for the following year.

What if, in reviewing your old tax returns, you discover that income averaging could have saved you money on one or more of them? You can file an amended return, Form 1040X, for any or all of the past three years. Attach a Schedule G to each 1040X you submit. The IRS will refund the excess taxes you paid, plus interest.

Using a Multiple Support Agreement to Claim an Extra Dependent

Are you missing the chance to take a $1,000 deduction? You may be if you're not claiming all of the dependents you're legally entitled to.

Under the tax law, you can claim someone as your dependent *if* he or she:

1. does not file a joint return;

2. is a U.S. citizen, resident, or national or resides in Canada or Mexico for some part of the year;

3. is either a member of your household, or a relative (like a son, daughter, parent, or grandparent);

4. has a gross income for the year of under $1,000 (not including social security benefits and other forms of tax-exempt income); and

5. receives more than 50 percent of his or her financial support from you.

The fifth requirement causes problems for many taxpayers. What if you do send money to a relative each month, but it doesn't add up to more than 50 percent of his or her support for the year? The answer is: File a Multiple Support Agreement.

Example: Your elderly mother lives an active but financially insecure life in another state. To help her make ends meet, you, your brother, and your brother-in-law each send her a monthly check. None of you alone provides more than 50 percent of her annual support. However, *one* of you can still claim her as a dependent and take a $1,000 deduction *if:*

1. she satisfies the first four requirements stated above;

2. each of you provides more than 10 percent of her support; and

3. together you provide more than 50 percent of her support.

Who gets the tax break? That's something you all have to decide together. My advice is to let the person who's in the highest tax bracket have it. That's who will benefit from it the most.

Let's say that you, your brother, and your brother-in-law agree to let your brother take the deduction this year. What now?

First, you will have to fill out an IRS Form 2120, Multiple Support Agreement. So will your brother-in-law. On it, you state that you will *not* claim your mother as a dependent on your tax return.

Next, you and your brother-in-law will have to give your completed forms to your brother. He in turn will have to attach these two forms to his return when he files. He can then claim your mother as his dependent and take the $1,000 deduction.

A Multiple Support Agreement must be renewed annually. If your brother wants to take this deduction again next year, he'll have to get new 2120 forms from both you and your brother-in-law. The same goes for the year after that, and for as long as the three of you keep supporting your mother.

What if you decide somewhere along the line that a different person in your group should take the deduction? There's no restriction stopping you from alternating. Just remember that the person who claims the dependent is the one who must file all of the paperwork.

Turning a Hobby into a Tax Break

You can find tax breaks in all kinds of places, if you only know where to look. Even a hobby can lead to some valuable tax deductions.

If you turn your hobby into a business, you're allowed to deduct your losses as long as you show a profit for any two or more years within a period of five consecutive years. (There's an exception to this rule: If your business involves horses, then you only have to be profitable for two out of seven years.)

Example: You enjoy picture framing, and you're always doing it for your family and friends. One day you decide to see if you can make some money at it. You stock up on materials and supplies, buy some new tools, and make improvements on your basement workroom. By the end of the year, you're almost ready to start taking customers.

What's the effect on that year's taxes? Even though you didn't earn a dime, you can deduct your expenses.

In January, you do a little advertising, word gets around, and before you know it your weekends are taken up with your framing business. Your expenses are still more than your income, but that's okay. When tax time rolls around again, you can deduct your expenses as long as you declare your income.

Where should you do this? On Schedule C, Profit or Loss from Business or Profession.

Caution: There's a little-known tax rule that can foul up the works if you're not prepared for it. The IRS can come in and say that you aren't serious about making a profit from your part-time business. They'll label it "an activity not engaged in for profit" and deny the losses you've claimed on your return.

You *can* argue that you're running a real business. And if you're able to convince them that you're not in it just for fun, you may get them to change their opinion.

The IRS will look carefully at your situation. These are some of the things they'll consider:

- What are your past profits and losses?
- If your profits are spotty, how much do you earn when the money does come in? (This issue can be very important if, for example, you're a writer who works freelance for years before landing a lucrative book contract.)
- How successful are you at your nine-to-five job?
- How much time and effort do you put into your sideline business?
- Do you handle yourself in a businesslike and professional manner?
- Do you actually *expect* to make a profit from what you do?
- Are you doing something that other people actually manage to make a living at, or are you mainly involved in your business for personal pleasure or recreation?

Example: Two adventurers who were not published authors chartered a boat and took an around-the-world cruise, claiming that they would later write a book about it. When they deducted their expenses, the IRS turned them down. And the Tax Court agreed with the IRS. They decided that the two had gone on their journey for pleasure, not business, and that their expenses were nondeductible hobby losses.

If you have a hobby that you've turned into a business, my advice is to make a small profit if at all possible. Try bunching a lot of costs into one year and delaying some of your income into the next to make that year more profitable. If you manage to show a profit at least twice and pay taxes on it, the IRS will have a hard time dismissing your part-time business as a hobby.

Self-Employment Taxes

It's tough to make a good living running your own business. Especially when the government takes almost 10 percent of your profits in the form of self-employment taxes.

Self-employment taxes are the equivalent of social security taxes paid out by employees and employers. The numbers are just different.

Example: For 1981 a self-employed businesswoman has to pay 9.3 percent in self-employment tax on the first $29,700 of her *net* income. That's $2,762.10. Anything she earns over the earnings base is free from this tax. Of course, she has to pay income taxes on all of her profits, too.

Example: A man who is employed by a large firm pays social security at the rate of 6.65 percent on the first $29,700 he earns. The most he has to pay for 1981 is $1,975.05.

His employer is required to match that figure, so the amount of social security that actually goes into his account is $3,950.10. But his own out-of-pocket contribution is $787.05 less than that of the self-employed businesswoman. That's quite a difference.

If you work for yourself and make a profit, you must file the long form, 1040, and attach Schedule SE, Computation of Social Security Self-Employment Tax. To figure your tax, just follow the form line by line.

There are two questions people commonly ask about the self-employment tax:

1. "How should I pay it?"

If you're self-employed and making a profit, you're supposed to make quarterly estimated tax payments. Simply include the self-employment taxes you currently owe in the same check you write to cover your income taxes. You don't have to write separate checks for each.

2. "What if I'm self-employed *and* hold down a regular job? Do I still have to pay self-employment taxes on all of my business profits?"

Maybe not. For 1981, only the first $29,700 in *combined* wages and self-employment earnings are subject to these taxes.

Example: You have a full-time job at a bank, and you also work as a financial consultant after hours and on weekends. During 1981, you earn $22,000 at your regular job and $12,000 from your consulting business, bringing your income for the year to a total of $34,000.

Because social security on the $22,000 you made at the bank was automatically withheld from your paychecks, you can subtract that from the $29,700 earnings base. The $7,700 difference is the amount you must pay self-employment taxes on. And since you earned more than that for your consulting work, the entire $7,700 is taxed at the 9.3 percent rate. Your self-employment tax bill for the year is $716.10.

Note: If your *net* self-employment income for the year is under $400, you don't have to pay this tax.

One Student May Be Worth Two Deductions

Is there a student in your family who holds down a job during the year? If so, then he or she can claim a $1,000 personal exemption on his or her own personal income tax return—*and* you as a parent may be able to claim the same $1,000 exemption on your return.

For your family to qualify for this double tax break, you must be able to claim the student as your dependent. Normally, you can claim someone as a dependent only if he or she:

1. does not file a joint return (in other words, he or she must file singly even if married);

2. is a U.S. citizen, resident, or national or resides in Canada or Mexico for some part of the year;

3. is either a relative or a member of your household;

4. receives more than 50 percent of his or her financial support from you; and

5. has a gross income for the year of under $1,000.

However, in the case of a student (or someone who's under the age of 19), rule number 5 simply doesn't apply. That's right. As long as a person meets the other four dependency requirements, you can claim him or her as a tax dependent, no matter how much he or she earns, and take the $1,000 exemption.

Under the tax law, there are two requirements a person must satisfy in order to be considered a student. Namely, he or she:

1. must be enrolled on a full-time basis in a qualified institution of higher education; and

2. must attend school for at least some part of five months out of the year (the months don't have to be consecutive, and going to school for even one day out of each month is enough to qualify).

Night school doesn't count.

Example: Your son attended your local college from January through May and again from September through December. He worked over Easter break, during summer vacation, and again over Christmas break, earning a total of $4,000 for the year.

As long as he meets the first four dependency requirements, you can go ahead and claim him as your tax dependent. And he can take the same $1,000 exemption on his own tax return, too.

Scholarships and Fellowships

With the costs of a good education going up each year, both students and parents welcome any financial assistance that comes their way. A scholarship or fellowship can make a big difference.

A scholarship is an amount awarded to a graduate or undergraduate student to help pay for his or her studies. Fellowships usually go to graduate or postgraduate students to assist them with further study and research.

Under the tax law, either type of grant can mean tax-free income. And it can be used to defray a number of expenses—including tuition, room, board, laundry, books, supplies, and incidental travel.

The tax law does make an important distinction between a student who is a degree candidate and one who isn't. For someone who is enrolled in a degree program, the entire amount of a scholarship or fellowship may be tax-free. But a nondegree candidate can only exclude a maximum of $300 a month from his or her income for up to 36 months.

This all sounds simple enough. So why have taxpayers and the IRS argued for years about scholarships and fellowships? Because some grants get tax-free treatment and some don't—and each new grant is unique.

To qualify for tax-free status, a grant must be given to further a student's education. That must be its *main* purpose. It can't be seen as benefiting the organization or school that gives it, nor can it take the form of compensation for something the student does.

For example: If your son is awarded an athletic scholarship, it's tax-free as long as his school doesn't require him to participate in a particular sport and won't cancel the grant if he can't participate. Or: Your daughter wins a beauty contest, and her prize package includes a college scholarship. Since it represents compensation for entering and winning the contest, it's taxable as income.

Public Health Service awards usually qualify as nontaxable scholarships. But Domestic Volunteer Service Awards are considered neither scholarships nor fellowships, and they're taxed.

What if you're not sure about whether a grant is tax-free? Contact the group that's giving it and ask them—they should know. If they don't, have your tax advisor check it out for you.

Family Estate Trusts

Many taxpayers handle their financial affairs through trusts of various kinds. The Marital Deduction Trust is commonly used in estate planning. Some business people and investors take advantage of the Clifford Trust when they want their property held for a period of time (ten years and one day). Testamentary trusts are often established in wills.

Most trusts are perfectly legal and make good tax sense. But there's one that's causing a lot of trouble these days: the Family Estate Trust.

Also known as a "constitutional trust," a "family equity trust," or a "pure trust," a Family Estate Trust is a clever scheme that may appear very attractive. But it really isn't. Here's a typical setup:

A promoter comes to you and, for a fee ranging anywhere from $2,500 to $25,000, shows you how to start your own Family Estate Trust. You put all of your assets into it. You also assign it all of your current and future income, your furniture, your car—in other words, everything you have. Of course, you are named the trustee.

Then you sit back and let the trust support you. It pays the mortgage on its house (where you live) and puts gas in its car (which you drive). It pays the premiums on the insurance policy it owns on your life. It buys the groceries (which you eat) for its table (where you sit).

The whole idea behind the trust is this: If all of your income goes to it, you don't have to report anything to the IRS or pay any taxes. And the trust ends up paying little or no tax.

It sounds very neat and tidy, but *it just doesn't work.* The IRS says so. The courts have repeatedly said so. All of the reputable tax professionals I've talked to say so.

If you try to use a Family Estate Trust, get ready for the IRS. You'll be assessed additional taxes, penalties, and interest. You may also be charged with negligence or even intentional tax evasion.

Vacation Homes

Do you own a cabin in the mountains or a cottage on the beach? Depending on what you do with it, your vacation home can either mean some nice tax benefits for you—or a big tax headache.

Here are the rules:

1. If you use your vacation property *only* for recreational purposes, you can deduct any real estate taxes and mortgage interest you pay on it. But that's all. In this case your vacation home is considered personal property, so you can't deduct upkeep, utilities, or depreciation.

Where should you claim these deductions? On Schedule A under "taxes" and "interest."

2. If you use your vacation property *only* as a source of rental income, you can still deduct your real estate taxes and mortgage interest. You can also deduct all of the costs associated with the ownership of income-producing property—like upkeep, utilities, and depreciation.

You'll have to report your rental income and deduct your expenses on Schedule E, Supplemental Income.

3. If you rent out your place part of the time and use it for your own enjoyment the other part, things get sticky.

The tax law says that if you use your vacation home for pleasure for more than 14 days out of the year, or a period equivalent to 10 percent of the time it's rented out (whichever is greater), you must restrict your income-producing property deductions. This involves some complicated rules and restrictions I don't want to go into here. If you're in this situation, my advice is to either study the published regulations yourself or consult with your tax advisor.

Note: Regardless of how you handle your vacation property, you can always take your real estate tax and mortgage interest deductions—in full.

One final point to keep in mind: If you rent out your vacation home for fewer than 15 days out of the year, you can pocket that income tax-free. The IRS considers this "incidental income," and they don't even want to know about it.

Barter

Bartering—the practice of trading goods and services— has received a great deal of publicity during the past few years. Part of this is due to the fact that it can occasionally lead to tax problems.

The official IRS position on this issue is that products or services traded through a barter agreement can result in income that must be reported.

Example: You're a piano teacher and your next-door neighbor is an electrician. He would like his son to take some lessons, and you need electrical circuits installed in the room you're adding on to your home. You decide to work out a trade.

According to the IRS, you should each figure out how much the services you receive are worth and include this figure in your income.

But the IRS isn't really that interested in bartering done on such a small scale. When it comes to organized barter clubs, though, they can get interested in a hurry. That's because some are set up in such a way that their members avoid reporting the value of the products and services they exchange.

Now, there's absolutely nothing wrong with belonging to an organized barter club. A lot of people find excellent values through these channels. There are many reputable barter clubs around these days, ranging from local groups with only a few members to national clubs that are used as clearinghouses.

If you're thinking of joining a barter club, first find out whether or not it will actually save you money. Then plan to report any goods or services you acquire through it as income on your tax return. That's the easiest way to stay out of trouble.

The Personal Use of a Company Car

If you have the use of a company car, congratulations! This is one of the nicest benefits around.

Until tax time, that is. The IRS is on the lookout for people who drive company-furnished automobiles. To you, it's a perquisite; to them, it may be a form of income.

Example: You drive a company car, and your firm picks up the tab for your gasoline, oil, and maintenance expenses. You use the car primarily for business-related driving. So far, so good.

But what about those times when you take the car out on personal errands, weekends, or evenings? According to the IRS, you're supposed to include the value of this type of use in your taxable income.

How much does that amount to? Probably about 20¢ a mile, as far as your company is concerned. They'll ask you to reimburse them at that rate for any personal driving you do in their car.

However, the IRS doesn't think this is enough. They claim that you should take the difference between the reimbursement you pay to your company and the actual value of your personal use of the car, and report this as taxable income.

They don't say what the "actual value" rate should be, though. And what about the fact that they'll only allow you to deduct 20¢ for each business mile you drive in your personal car, if you use their optional standard mileage rate? That's one of life's little ironies.

Confused? No wonder. Luckily, your company's accountants and tax people will usually take care of this matter for you. They'll work out whatever amount you should end up owing the IRS and add it to the "other compensation" column on your year-end W-2.

My advice is to continue reimbursing your company 20¢ a mile (or whatever rate they establish) for your personal driving. Report the "other compensation" as income on your tax return. This should satisfy the IRS.

Disability Income

If you've been away from your job for awhile because of an accident or illness, or if a disability has forced you to retire early, then you may feel as if you deserve some kind of tax break.

I have bad news for you. The IRS doesn't agree. In their eyes, most disability income is still income and therefore taxable.

Example: You miss work for three months because of an operation. You had accumulated some sick leave and vacation time before then, so you continue to receive your paychecks. Do you have to pay taxes on your earnings? Unfortunately, yes.

On the other hand, workmen's compensation is fully tax-exempt. The same goes for disability benefits you receive under a "no-fault" automobile insurance policy.

What if your disability is so bad that you have to retire? Again, the general rule is that you're supposed to report your retirement pension or annuity as income. Part of it may be tax-free; it all depends on who paid for your plan. If your employer funded it, it's taxable. But if you contributed to it, you may be able to exclude some portion of it from your income.

If you're not sure about how your own plan has been set up, talk with a knowledgeable company representative. He or she should be able to help you figure out what's taxable and what isn't.

If you discover that you do have to pay taxes on your disability income, you should consider taking the disability income exclusion. To qualify, you'll have to satisfy *all* of these requirements:

1. You must have been under 65 years old as of December 31, 1981; *and*

2. You can't have reached mandatory retirement age on January 1, 1981; *and*

3. You must have retired on disability; *and*

4. You must have been permanently and totally disabled when you retired; *and*

5. You can't have elected to treat your disability income as a regular pension or annuity.

I have more bad news. Even if you do qualify for this tax break, the most you can exclude from your income is $5,200. And if your adjusted gross income is $20,200 or more (you'll find that on line 31 of your 1040), you won't save any money at all.

Use IRS Form 2440, Disability Income Exclusion, to compute how much (if any) of your disability income is tax-exempt for 1981. Claim your exemption on line 28 of your 1040. Be sure to attach your Form 2440 when you file your return.

Alimony

A marital split can be emotionally and financially devastating. Children are bounced around. Property is divided. The family home may have to be sold. There are hard feelings all around.

Even in the midst of the turmoil surrounding a divorce or separation, both parties involved should be thinking about their taxes. That's because the IRS will be very interested in any money that changes hands, especially alimony.

Alimony can take three forms:

1. payments made under an official decree of divorce or separate maintenance, or under a written instrument incident to divorce or separation;

2. payments made under a written support agreement; and

3. payments made under a support decree.

The tax laws concerning alimony are fairly straightforward. If you pay it out, you can deduct your payments from your gross income on line 27 of your 1040. (You don't have to itemize on Schedule A in order to take this deduction.) If you receive it, on the other hand, you must report the payments as income on line 10 of your 1040. In any case, you do have to file the long form.

To be considered alimony—and qualify for the deduction—the payments must be classified as "periodic." This usually means that they must go on for more than 10 years. (In other words, a lump sum paid as part of a property settlement isn't deductible.)

Example: Under the terms of a written divorce decree, a husband agrees to pay $500 a month to his ex-wife for a period of 20 years. He gets to deduct the payments, and she has to report them on her tax return.

What happens if he gets behind in his payments? Then he

can deduct only what he actually paid during the year, and she has to report only what she actually received by year-end.

Some payments, while "periodic," still aren't alimony and can't be deducted.

Example: A man owed his ex-wife $40,000 as part of the property settlement. He wasn't able to pay the entire amount at once, so they agreed on $300 a month for a little over 11 years. He couldn't deduct the payments, and she didn't have to report them.

Alimony as a tax issue is reasonably clearcut. So is child support—it's neither deductible nor taxable. But what if a monthly payment is intended to cover both alimony *and* child support? Here's where a problem can arise.

Ideally, a divorce decree or written agreement will spell out what portion of a monthly payment will be designated alimony and what portion will go to child support. This makes it easier for everyone at tax time.

Unfortunately, not all couples who are undergoing a separation or divorce think this far ahead. A decree or agreement may not make this distinction. If it doesn't, then both parties have to treat the entire monthly payment as *alimony*—even if part of it is really meant as child support. That's what the law says.

Tax Shelters

Generally speaking, the IRS doesn't like tax shelters. Recently they've stepped up their fight against investments that result in excessive deductions and credits for taxpayers. In fact, they've established a special program for the purpose of identifying and prosecuting those persons who promote fraudulent tax shelters.

This doesn't mean that the IRS is opposed to *all* tax shelters. The IRS Commissioner has publicly stated that many investment opportunities are just fine. They make good financial as well as tax sense. And the deductions and credits they generate are okay as far as the IRS is concerned.

But the so-called "abusive" tax shelter is another story.

Example: You invest in some art prints that are valued at extraordinarily high prices. Your write-offs for depreciation and the investment tax credit are nowhere near reasonable, and there's almost no likelihood that your investment will ever be profitable (or even that you'll recoup the money you sank into it).

Is this the kind of tax shelter that will draw the IRS's attention? You can bet on it.

Even a conservative tax shelter may not be as wise an investment as it was in the past. That's because the top tax rate for individuals drops to 50 percent as of January 1, 1982. Before then, the IRS could take as much as 70¢ on the dollar from taxpayers in the higher income brackets. Under these circumstances, tax shelters seemed attractive. But now that you can keep at least half of every dollar you earn, it doesn't make much sense to put your money somewhere just so you can claim a tax loss.

Which tax shelters look promising at the moment? Investments in real estate and in oil and gas, to name a couple. Some farming and mining shelters, and even equipment leasing, are being offered by reputable organizations and may be worth looking into.

As is the case with any investment, you should approach a tax shelter very carefully and examine it from every angle. Don't focus only on the possible tax breaks.

Caution: Risky tax shelters tend to surface around November and December, when people are scurrying around trying to find last-minute deductions. You should never invest in a tax shelter on the spur of the moment. Good ones are available throughout the year, even during the first eight months. That's when you should be thinking about them, if ever.

How should you report a tax shelter on your return? That's not an easy question to answer because there are so many different types of shelters and setups around—corporations, limited partnerships, trusts, and so on. If you're not sure whether you can handle this yourself, get help from a professional tax advisor.

V.

HOW TO HANDLE
YOUR TAX RETURN

There's more to preparing and filing a tax return than meets the eye. A lot of people think that once they've figured their income and deductions, their work is nearly over. They're wrong.

The actual physical handling of your tax return— all the way from filling it in to sending it off—can make a big difference. A mistake or a misunderstanding on your part can draw attention to your return. It can even get you audited.

It's important to take the time and do it right. Why get caught on a technicality?

The Best Times to Fill Out
and File Your Tax Return

When should you start preparing your 1981 income tax return? As soon after the first of the year as you can. There are several reasons for not putting it off until later—and each could mean more money in your pocket:

1. If you organize your 1981 records in early January, you won't mix them up with receipts and papers from 1982.

2. You'll be less likely to lose important documents, like your final W-2 for 1981 and those little 1099 information slips reporting your dividend and interest income for that year.

3. You'll be able to tell exactly what records you have and what, if anything, you'll need before you can complete your return. And you'll have enough time to get duplicate copies of missing records, such as reports on the sale of securities (your stockbroker should have these). Be on the lookout for the annual statement from your mortgage company and inter- est statements from credit card companies, banks, stores you have charge accounts with, and savings and loan institu- tions.

Once you have all of your records in place, you can begin roughing out your return. Try to determine fairly quickly wheth- er you'll be claiming a refund or owing the IRS on April 15.

If it turns out that you're going to owe more tax than you've already paid, it's better to discover this early in the tax season. Then you can make plans to have enough money available in April to pay your tax bill in full.

When you're satisfied that your return is complete (and have checked it over for obvious errors), you have an impor- tant decision to make: When should you mail it?

Obviously, if you owe more taxes, you'll want to send in your return (and your check) as late as is legally possible. But what if you're due a refund? (Seventy-five to 80 percent of all individual taxpayers claim refunds on their returns.) The earlier you file, the sooner you'll get your check from the IRS. If you file in February or March, you can usually start expecting your refund within six to eight weeks.

However, there's another side to this issue. A growing number of tax professionals are saying that the later you file your return, the less your chances are of being audited. If you file early, they claim, your audit risk is increased.

The official word from the IRS is: They don't care when you file as long as you do it between January 1 and April 15. But if you file early in the season, it makes things a bit easier for them.

They also say that when you file doesn't make any differ- ence as far as their audit selection process is concerned. You can file early or late, and your return will stand the same chance of being picked for audit. There are many people who dispute this point, though.

In any case, you should fill out your return as soon as you can. When you actually mail it in is up to you.

Personally, I prefer to file my return close to the April 15 deadline. That's because I always end up owing a little money to the IRS, and I like to keep it as long as I can.

The Tax Package You Get from the IRS May Not Be What You Need

It's easy to tell when the tax season begins. That's when the IRS starts mailing out its tax packages. (They usually wait until the day after Christmas, so you'll probably receive yours around the first of the new year.)

A word of warning: You may think that your tax package will contain all of the forms and schedules you'll need to properly prepare your return. Chances are that it won't.

Example: Last year you filed the short form, 1040A. This year you want to file the long form, 1040, and take advantage of such deductions as contributions to your IRA account, alimony payments, and moving expenses. But what you get in the mail from the IRS is the short form.

That's because the IRS determines what forms to send you each year on the basis of the last return you filed.

Example: Last year you filed the long form, itemized your deductions on Schedule A, and reported $500 in dividend and interest income on Schedule B. That's all. Your return was relatively straightforward.

However, this year's return is another story. You've decided to income average (you'll need Schedule G), deduct mileage expenses associated with your full-time job that weren't reimbursed by your employer (Form 2106), and deduct a small partnership loss you sustained from an oil and gas venture (Schedule E). You also want to report income from a sideline business you started (Schedules C and SE). Finally, you sold your home at a profit last year and bought a more expensive one, and you want to defer paying tax on the gain (Form 2119 and Schedule D).

[87]

Obviously, the tax package the IRS sends you won't be sufficient. It's up to you to make up a tax package of your own.

Go to your local IRS office and pick up any additional forms you need. Don't be surprised if all of the forms aren't available in January; many IRS offices won't have full supplies until February or even later. If you don't want to wait (and you probably shouldn't), check with your tax preparer. He or she will more than likely have at least one copy of each form and can make photocopies for you.

In any case, don't ask the IRS to mail you the forms you need. Things are hectic during the filing season, and they're bound to be rushed. Your request may be delayed or lost altogether. And the IRS won't accept as an excuse for late filing your plea that you didn't have the proper forms.

Note: You may not even receive a tax package in the mail this year. The IRS tries to send forms to everyone who filed during the previous year, but they can't always manage to do it. And if you're newly divorced, or if you moved recently and the IRS doesn't have your current address, then you probably won't get a package from them.

You May Not Even Need to File

Before you start thinking about your tax return, you should determine whether you need to file at all. That's right. You may be able to avoid the aggravation entirely.

Here are the rules:

1. If you're single and your gross income for 1981 was less than $3,300, you don't have to file. If you're 65 or older, the ceiling rises to $4,300.

2. If you're married and your combined income was less than $5,400, you don't have to file. If either you or your spouse is 65 or older, the limit rises to $6,400; if you're both 65 or older, it jumps to $7,400.

3. If you're self-employed, you don't have to file if your *net* earnings were under $400. (Your net earnings are your bottom-line profits after all expenses have been taken out.)

But if you owe some self-employment or social security taxes, you'll have to complete a return and send it along with your tax payment.

What if you have a refund coming? You'll have to file a return asking for it; the IRS won't send it to you automatically. Be sure to keep this in mind if you worked part-time in 1981 and taxes were withheld from your paychecks, or if you're retired and taxes were withheld from your pension checks.

Note: A lot of parents whose children have unearned income (dividends and interest) aren't sure about when they're supposed to file for them. Here's the rule: If your child's unearned income is less than $1,000, you're not required to file a return for him or her. But you may want to anyway. That's because the IRS receives 1099 forms reporting the interest or dividends your child is paid. If they don't find a tax return to match against those 1099s, they'll want to know where it is, and they'll send you a letter.

To prevent this from happening, simply file a return for your child reporting the interest or dividend income and showing that it's under the limit.

The Long Form or the Short Form: Which Is Best for You?

There's no question that it's simpler to file the short form, 1040A, than the long form, 1040. In 1980, more than 37.6 million taxpayers—40 percent of all taxpayers who filed personal returns—used the short form.

But too many people have the wrong idea about the short form. The fact is that taking the easy way out can cost you extra tax dollars. That's because the long form allows for many important tax benefits that aren't listed on the 1040A.

There are times when you *must* file the long form. If you had income from pensions or annuities, sold your home, earned self-employment income, or received alimony, then you will have to use the long form. If you want to deduct job-related moving expenses, employee business costs, IRA or Keogh retirement plan contributions, or alimony payments, you will have to file the long form. Ditto if you paid a prema- ture withdrawal penalty for cashing in a certificate of deposit early.

People who income average, claim residential energy tax credits, or get an extension of time to file their return must also use the long form. However, the political contributions credit and the earned income credit for lower income families may be taken on either the 1040 or the 1040A.

Recommendation: You should *always* consider filing the long form. There is absolutely no way this can hurt you. Filing the short form *can* and *will*, though, if there are additional deductions and credits you should be taking.

Many people have what they think is a perfect excuse for not filing the long form: They don't have enough in itemized deductions on Schedule A. (Schedule A of the Form 1040 is where you claim your medical bills, real estate and other taxes, interest, charitable contributions, casualty losses, and miscellaneous items.) To itemize, a married couple filing jointly must have at least $3,400 in itemized deductions before the next dollar in deductions does any good. Singles and those claiming head-of-household filing status need $2,300 in item- ized deductions. Married couples filing separately need $1,700 for each spouse.

But even if you *don't* have enough expenses to itemize on Schedule A, you should *still* file the long form to take advan- tage of the other deductions I mentioned earlier—like IRA contributions, alimony payments, moving costs, and insulation expenses. You can't deduct these on the short form.

I know a number of people who always assumed that they were better off filing the short form. But after checking into it, they found that the long form would have saved them more tax dollars.

If this is true for you, my advice is to file an amended return on Form 1040X for each year you want to change. This form allows you to "switch" from the short form to the long form and claim missed deductions. And don't worry—this is not the sort of thing that will cause the IRS to audit your tax records.

How far back can you go? Generally speaking, three years. For example, you have until April 15, 1982 (the due date of your 1981 return) to file a 1040X for your 1978 return. You have until April 15, 1983 to make changes on your 1979 return—and so on.

You Can File without Your W-2

Contrary to popular belief, you can file your income tax return even if you're missing your W-2. That's the form that reports your annual salary and wages and the amounts withheld from your paychecks for social security and federal, state, and local income taxes.

Most employers get W-2s out to their employees by the January 31 deadline required by law. But sometimes a hitch develops along the way.

For example: You changed jobs last June. Your old employer gave you your W-2 in July—and you lost it. Or: You receive your W-2 on time, but it's incorrect. It may take weeks or even longer to have it fixed. You have a refund coming, though, so you want to file your return immediately. Or: The company you work for is just plain late in getting the forms out. "The computers are down," or some such excuse.

The official word from the IRS is that you should always include your W-2 with your tax return. If you don't receive it by January 31, you're supposed to go to your employer and ask for it. If you do receive it and it's wrong, you're supposed to ask your employer to correct it. And if things aren't in order by February 15, you're supposed to call the IRS and let them know.

But what if you really want to get moving on your return? My advice is to start preparing it even without your W-2.

Look at your final earnings statement for 1981. It may show your total earnings and withholding as of year-end.

Or go back through all of your old pay stubs and add up the figures. You should be able to determine how much you earned and how much you paid in withholding.

If you haven't received your W-2 by the time you're ready to mail your return, you'll have two options:

1. You can wait for your W-2 and file when you get it. If you're claiming a refund, this will delay it somewhat. Or:

2. You can go ahead and file without your W-2. You'll need to attach a note to your return explaining why it's missing, along with a correct year-end earnings statement. This should be enough to satisfy the IRS and enable them to process your return and your refund.

In general, though, filing without a W-2 isn't a terrific idea. You shouldn't do it unless you feel it's absolutely necessary.

What if you owe the IRS and you don't get your W-2 early in the tax season? Don't be in a hurry to file. Wait until you receive your form; you should get it in time to mail your return by April 15. If for some reason you don't, of course, you'll *have* to file without it—or pay late filing penalties.

Rounding Off to the Nearest Whole Dollar

Personal income taxes can get pretty complicated. That's why you should do whatever you can to simplify your return and its preparation.

Want to make your computations easier? Then eliminate the pennies on your return by rounding figures off to the nearest whole dollar. Just keep these three rules in mind along the way:

1. Numbers between 1–49¢ can be rounded down; numbers between 50–99¢ should be rounded up.

2. Be consistent. If you decide to round off your figures, do so on *all* of the forms and schedules you file.

3. Don't round off the amounts on your receipts before totaling them. For example, add all of your medical bills together down to the last penny. Then round off this final figure to get the number you'll list on your return.

Some tax professionals feel that you shouldn't round off because the IRS likes precision. Reporting every amount in dollars and cents shows how meticulous you are.

My advice is to go ahead and round off if you want to. It will save you time and headaches. I've never heard of the IRS selecting a return for audit just because of rounding, nor have

I heard of an auditor who will accept a taxpayer's word about a return simply because every penny received or deducted has been listed.

Should You Attach Notes to Your Return?

Should you attach notes to your return explaining some of the "funny-looking" items? As a general rule, the answer is a resounding NO!

Now it's true that everyone's income tax return is personal and unique. And almost everyone is absolutely certain that his or her return is going to be selected for audit when, in fact, less than 2 percent of all returns filed in 1982 will ever be seriously questioned. People think that writing notes and stapling them to their forms will help them to avoid an audit, but this isn't the case. It can actually work *against* them by drawing unnecessary attention to their returns.

However, there are times when you will need to attach explanations, such as when you make charitable donations of extremely valuable property. If you *must* write a note, here's how to go about doing it:

1. Put an asterisk beside the questionable area on your form and add a notation to "see attached explanation."

2. Keep the note itself short and to the point, don't get carried away and write a thesis. One or two paragraphs is usually more than enough.

Example: "Taxpayer is deducting $9,000 in medical costs paid to orthodontist for three members of the family. No expenses were reimbursed by insurance or otherwise. All expenses were paid during the tax year."

Remember that the idea behind an explanatory note is to satisfy the curiosity of the first person who sees your return after the computer has picked it out for scrutiny. A note should *not* make the IRS more interested.

3. Don't use a note as an excuse to argue technicalities. All it should include is verification of how you treated a particular item on your return.

4. Never, ever include a big sheaf of documents and receipts with your return.

Some taxpayers feel that every section of their return is going to set off all the bells and whistles on the IRS computer. They're wrong. My advice is to explain only those items that you are absolutely, 100-percent sure will cause the computer to select your return.

The bottom line is this: When in doubt, don't do it. If you do get called in for an audit on one or two questionable items, that's really the proper time to explain yourself—not when you file.

An Incomplete Return Could Delay Your Refund

Before you mail your tax return, take a few moments to look it over. Make absolutely sure that you've checked all the necessary boxes, filled in all the lines, and attached all the forms and schedules you're supposed to. A simple omission could delay your refund check for weeks or even months.

The IRS has been known to hold on to a $1,000 or $2,000 refund because a single question on a return went unanswered. If your return is incomplete, the IRS will send you a note asking about the missing answer, form, or schedule. And they may put off processing your return—and your refund—until they hear from you.

Even worse, they might decide that you deliberately left your return unfinished. If they do, they'll not only delay your refund but may also assess you harsh penalties. However, this doesn't happen very often. The only people they really want to penalize are the tax protesters, some of whom do file incomplete returns on purpose. Most of us make an honest effort to fill out our returns completely, and the IRS realizes this.

Still, it's easy to overlook one or two items. Here are some that taxpayers commonly miss:

1. Schedule B, Part III.

If you have more than $400 in dividends or interest to report to the IRS and you're filing the long form, 1040, you must also file Schedule B. At the bottom of this form is a series of questions concerning foreign bank and trust accounts. Even though you may not have accounts in other countries (most people don't), you have to answer these questions anyway.

2. Residential energy tax credits (Form 5695).

The first question on this form asks when your home was "substantially completed." If it was built after April 20, 1977, you're not allowed to take the regular energy tax credit. Failure to answer this question could delay your whole return.

3. The credit for child and dependent care expenses (Form 2441).

At the bottom of this form, the IRS asks if you filled out the necessary wage returns for household workers who performed services in your home. This is primarily for parents who hire people to come into their homes and care for their children. But even if you took your children to a day care center, you have to answer this question or the IRS could hold up your return.

Recommendation: To be on the safe side, always fill in each and every line on your return. Put a "0" or a dash next to those items that don't apply to you.

You don't *have* to do this, but it can't hurt. It will show the IRS that you've at least considered all of the questions, and it will lower your risk of having your return delayed because of an oversight.

Avoid Making Obvious Errors on Your Return

No matter how careful you are when doing your taxes or how good your records look, you probably still worry that your return will stick out like a red flag, begging for closer scrutiny by the IRS. Calm down. You'll feel better at mailing time if you carefully make one last check of your return for what I call "obvious" errors. These are items that are guaranteed to draw the IRS's attention.

In 1980, more than 6 percent of all taxpayers filing the short form, 1040A, made math errors on their returns. The error rate for the long form, 1040, was 7.5 percent. Take the time to review your addition and subtraction.

Some taxpayers whose income is below $10,000 forget to claim the earned income credit. The IRS considers this an error.

Some taxpayers forget to pay their quarterly estimated tax bills on time throughout the year. If you owe the IRS more than $100 at year-end and don't attach Form 2210, Underpayment of Estimated Tax by Individuals, to your personal return explaining the situation, the IRS will send you a bill for underpaying your estimated taxes.

Some taxpayers figure their tax correctly down to the last line and then use the wrong tax table. For example: A single person inadvertently uses the "married, filing jointly" table.

Another easy-to-spot error involves neglecting to take the 3 percent limit into account when deducting your medical expenses.

The IRS also looks for returns claiming deductions that seem logical but just aren't allowed under the law.

For example: You can't claim a partial dependency exemption for your mother-in-law who lives with you for half a year. (The IRS doesn't allow partial dependency exemptions.) You can't deduct federal income taxes or social security taxes withheld from your paychecks as itemized deductions on Schedule A. You can't deduct auto licenses and tags for your personal car, or fishing and hunting licenses.

You're not permitted to deduct personal living expenses or commuting expenses. Or a loss on the sale of your home. A casualty loss from termites isn't deductible. Neither are contributions to lobbying organizations or foreign charities, or the monetary value of any time or labor you spend as a volunteer.

If your return does not contain any obvious errors like these, the IRS will probably process it, mail you your refund (if you're claiming one), and that will be the end of it.

But what if you do make a mistake somewhere? One of two things can happen:

1. If you're asking for a refund, the IRS will simply adjust your return. This adjustment will be reflected on your refund check. They'll also send you a separate letter explaining the change. If your refund doesn't turn out to be what you expected, wait to hear from them before taking any action.

2. If you owe the IRS and you make an error in computing your taxes, the IRS will send you a notice and a bill for the amount of your mistake.

Don't worry; this isn't an audit. All the IRS wants is more of your money. If they're right, send your money by the due date they specify. But if you think they're wrong (and this happens frequently), you'll have the opportunity to state your case.

Never Let the IRS Keep Your Refund

If you file the short form, 1040A, and claim a refund, the IRS will send you a check for that amount (provided you haven't made any errors on your return). But if you file the long form, 1040, they offer you an alternative to getting a check from them. On line 65, they ask if you want to let them keep your refund and apply it to your 1982 estimated tax bill.

Don't do it! My advice it to *never, ever* let the IRS hold on to your refund.

Why not? Because it won't really help you in the long run—and it may end up hurting you.

Example: You fill out your 1981 return and discover that you have a $900 refund coming. You decide to let the IRS hold on to it and apply it to your 1982 tax bill.

But what if the IRS finds a math error on your return? Or your employer made a mistake on your wage statement? Or you forgot to include in your income the interest you earned on a bank account?

Any one of these things *could* happen. And any one of them would affect your tax return.

Let's suppose that the bottom line is this: After correcting your return, the IRS sends you a bill for an additional $400.

You already have $900 sitting in your estimated tax account. As far as you're concerned, they can go ahead and take the $400 out of that. Right?

Wrong. You told them to credit the $900 to your 1982 tax bill, and you're stuck with that decision. In other words, you'll have to come up with the extra $400 on your own.

What if the IRS audits your 1980 return and finds that you

owe additional taxes plus interest? You still can't touch your $900.

To make matters worse, the money you left in your estimated tax account doesn't even earn any interest. At today's high rates, that's $135 in interest you could be collecting.

If you really want to earmark your refund for your 1982 tax bill, let the IRS send you your check. Then deposit the money in a savings account or invest it for a year. Don't let the IRS have it for nothing.

How to Handle Your Tax Payments

If you ever find that you owe money to the IRS, take this debt seriously. Handle your payment in a businesslike manner. File all of the necessary forms and send them to the proper IRS Service Center—on time. And don't try any tricks. They usually won't work.

Example: When filling out his 1979 return, one taxpayer found that he owed additional income taxes. He made out a personal check for less than the full amount owed and wrote across the back, "Income Taxes Paid In Full." Very funny. The IRS simply cashed his check and sent him a bill for the balance due.

Whenever you send a payment to the IRS, be sure to write the following three things on the face of your check:

1. your social security number (or employer identification number, if you're paying withholding taxes for your employees);

2. the proper tax form number (1040 if the payment applies to your individual return; 501 for payroll tax deposits); and

3. the tax year and quarter or month for which the payment is being made.

This information will help the IRS to credit your payments correctly. Without it, they'll follow their own procedure— which may not be what you want. They'll use your check to cover your oldest outstanding tax bill, then any penalties and interest that apply to it, then your next oldest tax bill, and so on.

Example: You're ready to mail in your 1981 return, and you owe additional taxes. Recently the IRS audited your 1979 return and determined that you owe more taxes, a 5 percent negligence penalty, and interest for that year.

You mail your 1981 return along with a check covering the amount due for 1981. But you don't indicate on your check that the money should be used to pay your 1981 tax bill. So the IRS applies your check to the balance due on your 1979 return and then to the penalties and interest they charged you for that year. If there's anything left over, it goes toward your 1981 tax bill.

In other words, your 1981 payment is short, even though that's not what you intended.

You should always earmark your payments for specific tax bills so this sort of thing doesn't happen. You get to tell the IRS exactly which year your check is meant to cover and how you want it applied.

Caution: If you're paying withholding taxes for your employees, you don't have this option. The IRS will use your money to cover your oldest outstanding payroll tax bill first.

By the way, the interest you pay on a tax deficiency is deductible in the year it's paid. If you're paying off old tax bills that include interest, indicate on your check that you want the interest to be paid first. Then you'll be able to increase your interest deduction for the year.

You Can Get More Time to File Your Tax Return

It's a well-known fact that the IRS requires most people to file their individual income tax returns by April 15 each year. However, there are exceptions to this rule. If you need—or simply want—additional time to file, you can get it.

How? With IRS Form 4868, Application for Automatic Extension of Time to File U.S. Individual Income Tax Return. Most IRS offices have copies; so do tax preparers. As the title says, this extension is automatic. It gives you an extra 60 days in which to file.

It does *not*, repeat *not*, give you an extra 60 days to pay any taxes you might owe. Those are still due by April 15.

If that's the case, why would you want to file for an extension? Maybe you don't have all of the records you need to complete your return. Or maybe you don't have time to do it. Or maybe your finances are so complicated that you really need the extra two months to pull things together.

Whatever your reason, the IRS will grant you this extension as long as you do the following three things:

1. List on your Form 4868 the total amount of your 1981 tax bill, the amount of income withheld from your paychecks during the year, and/or any estimated tax payments you made.

2. Estimate how much, if anything, you still owe the IRS, and write them a check.

3. Mail the completed form, along with your check, by April 15 to the IRS Service Center where you'll eventually be filing your return.

You may be wondering how you can figure out your tax bill (and calculate how much you might owe) without first completing your return. You can't—not down to the last dollar. But the IRS does require you to make the best guess possible.

If your estimate turns out to be within 90 percent of your final tax bill, you're okay. If it falls under that limit, you'll have to pay penalties when you file in June.

Example: You file for an extension and send the IRS your check for $4,500, which you feel will cover your outstanding 1981 tax bill. Later, when you finish your return, you discover that you should have sent in $5,000—$500 more than you'd originally thought. No problem; your guess was within the 90 percent limit, and you'll send in the $500 with your return by June 14. Be sure to enter your $4,500 payment on line 58 of your 1040 so you'll get credit for it. Also attach a copy of the Form 4868 to your return.

If you end up overestimating your taxes on Form 4868 and overpaying the IRS, simply claim a refund when you file.

Recommendation: If you do decide to get an extension, try to have your Form 4868 ready to go a week or two before the April 15 deadline. Then you won't get caught in the last-minute panic at the post office.

What if you need even more time than the extension allows? You may be able to get it. Unlike your first extension, though, a second one will by no means be automatic.

You'll have to write to the IRS and explain why you can't finish your return by June 14. The only excuses they will accept are those which stem from circumstances beyond your control. For example: Your tax preparer died or is seriously ill. Or: Your securities transactions during 1981 were so numerous and complex that you can't get everything analyzed by the middle of June.

These are reasons the IRS will understand. If yours aren't as good, you'd better plan to file by June 14.

Should You Use the Preprinted Labels and Envelopes?

For some reason, many taxpayers are nervous about using the preprinted labels and envelopes they receive in the tax packages mailed out by the IRS. They're afraid that these materials contain information that can red flag a return for an audit.

Personally, I believe the IRS when they say there's nothing on these labels and envelopes that will automatically cause your return to be singled out.

The label usually contains your name (and that of your spouse, in the case of a joint return), address, and zip code. At the top is your social security number (or numbers, if you're filing jointly). There's also a designation of the district from which you're filing.

The envelope is coded with the number of your tax form (1040, for most individuals) and your geographical area. That's about all.

The IRS wants you to use their labels and envelopes. Practically speaking, it helps them if you do. If you choose not to, it takes the IRS a bit more time and trouble to process your return.

My advice is to go ahead and use these preprinted materials *unless:*

1. you *really* don't want to (there's no law saying you have to); or

2. the label contains inaccurate information. If this is the case, simply tear it up and throw it away. Then enter your name, address, and social security number on the face of your tax form.

The IRS tells you to correct any mistakes on the label and use it anyway. I disagree. It's too easy for them to overlook handwritten changes.

Last-Minute Filing Tips

If you wait until the very last minute to finish up your return and get it in to the IRS, you'll probably join the parade down to the post office to beat the midnight filing deadline. Here are a few final tips:

1. Don't run your envelope through a postage meter. Use stamps. The IRS looks for proof of the mailing date on all returns received after April 15. They don't accept postage meter imprints because meters are too easy to backdate.

2. If possible, have the stamps on your tax return hand cancelled—legibly—to prove that you got your return in on time.

3. If you're really nervous about proving your mailing date, spend the $1-$2 it takes to send your return to the IRS Service Center by certified mail, return receipt requested. This will not only prove absolutely that you mailed your return on time but will also give you verification that the IRS received it.

In any case, be sure to mail your return yourself. Don't trust someone else to drop it off at the post office for you. If your delivery person fouls up, it's still your fault if your return is late. Don't even trust your accountant to mail it for you.

If you haven't yet finished your return and midnight is fast approaching, my advice is to postpone sending it in. I've found that when people work right up to the deadline, they tend to get sloppy. They overlook legitimate deductions and other tax breaks (like income averaging) just so they can get their return done and mailed on time.

Instead of paying more taxes than necessary, file IRS Form 4868, Application for Automatic Extension of Time to File U.S. Individual Income Tax Return. Fill out this short form and send it to the IRS by midnight on April 15, along with your check for any outstanding taxes, and the IRS will give you an extra 60 days to file your return. (If you owe the IRS and you don't mail them a check along with this form, they won't allow the extension.)

You'll then have until June 14 to file your 1981 return. With the pressure off, you'll be able to take everything you have coming to you.

If you owe the IRS and you're late in filing your 1981 return, you'll be slapped with a penalty of 5 percent of the tax due for each month or part of a month during which you fail to file. The maximum penalty for late filing is 25 percent.

If you're late in paying, the IRS will charge you a penalty of one-half of 1 percent of the unpaid tax for each month or part of a month that your bill is outstanding. Again, the maximum penalty is 25 percent.

Recommendation: If you owe but don't have the money to pay, file your return anyway At least you'll avoid the stiff late filing penalty.

On top of the penalties I've just listed, the IRS also charges interest on the amount of your unpaid balance.

Now for some good news.

What most people don't realize about this last-minute filing madness Is that the April 15 deadline affects *only* those who *owe* the IRS. In other words, if you're due a refund and you're late getting your return in, there's no penalty the IRS can charge you. That's right. If they owe you, they can't penalize you for mailing your return in May, June, or even later. All penalties and interest charged by the IRS are based on unpaid balances owed to them.

That's why I've never really understood why everyone runs down to the post office at midnight on April 15. Most taxpayers filing individual returns—77 percent, in fact—are asking the IRS for refunds.

If you're claiming a refund and you don't have your return completed by the April 15 deadline, relax. Take a few extra days and do it right.

VI.

WILL YOU BE AUDITED?

No one likes to think about the possibility of an IRS audit. Yet everyone who files a tax return stands the chance of being audited.

There's no guarantee that your return will sail smoothly through the system, no matter how careful you are. But unless you do something illegal, you really shouldn't worry too much.

Our tax system is the best in the free world. Even the IRS agrees that we're basically honest people. In other words, you probably won't be audited—not this year, and maybe not ever. Still, it doesn't hurt to be prepared.

What's Your Audit Risk?

Too many people spend too much time worrying about the possibility of being audited. For the most part, their fears are unfounded. The IRS receives somewhere around 90 million individual income tax returns annually. Of these, only about 2 percent are ever audited. And this figure seems to be dropping slightly every year.

What determines whether or not you'll end up in that unlucky 2 percent? A lot of things—like the type of return you file, your income level, the kinds of deductions you take, and even where you live.

If you file a personal individual income tax return on Form 1040 or 1040A, and your income is under $10,000, the chances of your being audited are less than 1 percent. If your income is between $15,000 and $50,000, that rises to 2.5 percent. But if you make over $50,000 a year, it jumps to 8.5 percent.

If you own your own business, and the business income you report on Schedule C is between $10,000 and $30,000 a year, your audit risk is under 2 percent. If your business income is more than $30,000, make that 5 percent.

If you report both salary and self-employment income, the IRS will decide whether to classify your return as primarily personal or primarily business. They'll look to see which provides your major source of income, your job or your business. If, for example, your personal income is $55,000 and you earn another $15,000 a year from a small sideline business, the IRS will classify your return as personal. Your audit risk will be 8.5 percent rather than 5 percent.

If you get a refund, does this mean that you won't be audited? Not necessarily. On the other hand, the size of your refund won't affect your audit risk at all. A refund of $5,000 is no more likely to alarm the IRS than a $50 one.

What if you need an extension of time to file? Don't be afraid to ask for it—it won't up your chances of being audited. As long as you meet the extension deadline, the IRS won't treat your return any differently than those filed by April 15.

Strangely enough, the percentage of returns selected for audit varies quite a bit from one region of the country to another. If you live in Boston, your overall chances are about 1.3 percent. But if you live in Los Angeles, they're 3.4 percent. What about Dallas, Texas? 1.6 percent. Manhattan? 3.2 percent.

How you handle your deductions and credits can affect your audit potential. If you claim higher-than-average deductions for charitable donations, business and travel expenses, country club dues, a vacation home, or an office in your home, your audit risk will increase. But don't let this stop you from taking deductions you're entitled to.

The IRS frowns on abusive tax shelters. If you invest in one, your chances of being audited are about one in four.

If you're identified as a tax protester—mistakenly or otherwise—your risk takes a giant leap to 100 percent. The IRS goes after tax protesters.

What's the bottom line? If you're as honest as you can be on your tax return, you probably don't have anything to worry about. As long as you're not doing anything illegal, your chances of being audited are pretty slim.

The Average Deductions: Where Do You Fit In?

Once the IRS receives your tax return, they check it to make sure that you did your adding and subtracting correctly and didn't make any obvious errors. If they don't find any thing wrong, they usually go ahead and process your refund, if you have one coming.

Your return is then automatically screened by the IRS's computers for its audit potential. Everyone's return is. This doesn't necessarily mean that you'll be audited—only that your forms and schedules will be compared with the ones your friends and neighbors filed. If your figures come out close to the averages, that will probably be the end of it.

The further away from these averages you are, though, the higher your chances of being audited. That's because the IRS has found that out-of-sync returns tend to yield additional tax dollars. Three out of four of all returns picked for audit are chosen for that reason alone.

It helps to be aware of these averages and compare your own return against them. This serves two purposes:

1. It gives you some idea of your audit risk. If your figures are way out of line on the high side, you may be a prime candidate for selection by the IRS's computer.

2. It may clue you in to tax breaks you're missing. If your figures are really low in some areas, it may mean that you're overlooking important deductions and credits.

The table shown here lists the average deductions taken by taxpayers on returns filed by April 15, 1980.

AVERAGE DEDUCTIONS AND TAX CREDITS BY ADJUSTED GROSS INCOME

Adjusted Gross Income	$20,000-$25,000	$25,000-$30,000	$30,000-$40,000	$40,000-$50,000	$50,000-$75,000	$75,000-$100,000
Medical Expenses	600	550	500	500 _893_	650	800
Taxes Paid	1,700	2,000	2,500	3,300 _3124_	4,600	6,600
Interest Paid	2,600	2,800	3,100	3,600 _2,437_	4,700	6,600
Charitable Contributions	600	650	800	1,000 _893_	1,550	2,600
Miscellaneous Deductions	500	500	600	700 /	1,000	1,500
Residential Energy Tax Credit	90	100	100	110	130	145
TOTAL TAX LIABILITIES	$3,000	$4,000	$5,600	$8,500	$14,000	$24,000
Total Itemized Deductions as Percentage of Adjusted Gross Income	25%	22%	20%	19.5%	19.5%	19%

Caution: You should never, *ever* claim the average deductions on your own return unless they reflect exactly what you spent on tax deductible items. The table is not a license to take deductions you don't deserve. Use it only to see where you fit in.

According to the table, if you were an average taxpayer in 1980 and your adjusted gross income was $20,000–$25,000, you claimed $600 in medical expenses, paid out $1,700 in deductible taxes and $2,600 in interest, and gave $600 to charity. After you added in some miscellaneous items, your total itemized deductions came to about 25 percent of your adjusted gross income. And your tax bill for the year was right around $3,000.

If your adjusted gross income was between $40,000 and $50,000, your medical costs were about $500, you paid out $3,300 in deductible taxes and $3,600 in interest, and you gave $1,000 to charity. Your total itemized deductions amounted to approximately 19.5 percent of your adjusted gross income, and your tax bill for the year was around $8,500.

As you compare your own return to these averages, don't worry if your figures aren't exactly the same as the ones listed under your adjusted gross income level. If you fall somewhere within the general range, you should be okay.

Pay special attention to the percentages on the bottom line of the table. As your adjusted gross income increases, the overall *amount* of your Schedule A deductions should also increase. But they should amount to a *lower percentage* of your adjusted gross income.

Note: Never avoid deducting an item or two just because it's going to up your percentage. For example, if you purchased a home during the past two years, your mortgage interest payments and real estate taxes are high right now. You should go ahead and deduct them even though they'll put you above the averages. You'll have all the proof you'll need if you're ever called in to verify these deductions.

The IRS Matching Program: How Good Is It?

Last year, taxpayers filed between 140 and 150 million returns of all types, including 90 million individual returns. The IRS received an additional 500 million bits and pieces of information on wages, dividends, interest, and other income. And they processed more than 70 million refund checks.

You'd think that the IRS would be swamped with paperwork. As a matter of fact, they are. Yet they're *very* efficient when it comes to comparing the income you report on your return with the data they receive on you from various sources, like your employer and your bank.

The IRS's matching program is good—no question about it. They match almost every W-2 they get against its corresponding tax return. In 1980, together with the Social Security Administration, they processed information on some 189 million wage reports. If you were paid any salary at all during the year that was subject to income tax and social security withholding, you can bet that the IRS knows about it. If they can't find that income on your tax return, you'll get a letter.

What about those little 1099s reporting dividend and interest income? In 1980, the IRS received 350 million of them. About 303 million came in on computer tapes, and almost all of those were matched against returns. But of the remaining 43 million, which arrived as slips of paper, only 20-25 percent were checked.

If you have income from dividends, interest, wages, freelance or contract work, or even odd jobs, my advice is to report it. All of it.

What if you forget to report something? The IRS will probably send you a letter asking about the difference between the figures on your return and the figures they have on record. If it seems as if you made an honest mistake that could have happened to anyone, they'll just send you a bill for the back taxes you owe. Pay it as soon as you can, and you shouldn't have any problem.

Is It Risky to File an Amended Return?

Did you just find out about a tax break you've overlooked until now? Could it have saved you money on, for example, your 1979 return? If so, then by all means file an amended return and ask the IRS to refund the excess taxes you paid. It's that simple.

Unfortunately, too many taxpayers refuse to do this. They're afraid that filing an amended return will automatically get them audited. But that's *not* the way the system works.

If you send in an amended return, of course the IRS will screen it. They'll want to see if your claim is reasonable. And then, unless you're way off base, they'll process your return and send you your refund check, plus interest.

In other words, there's no excuse for not filing an amended return if you think the IRS owes you money. It isn't risky, and it isn't that hard to do.

For each return you want to change, you'll need a Form

1040X. Follow the instructions on it. You'll have to take some information from the earlier return, explain to the IRS why you feel the amendment is proper, give them your new figures, and tell them how much of a refund you're claiming. Use the tax forms and tables from that year. If you didn't save yours, ask your tax advisor or preparer for copies. He or she will probably have them available.

How far back can you go? In general, three tax years. You can file an amended return for the 1978 tax year if you do it by April 15, 1982—the due date of your 1981 return.

There are many reasons to file amended returns. For example: You're married, and you and your partner have always filed separately. You discover that you could have saved money if you'd filed jointly. Or: Your income has been up one year, down the next. You hear about income averaging, and it sounds like a good idea. Or: You usually file the short form. But now you realize that you could have deducted your IRA contributions, alimony payments, and expenses associated with a job-related move if only you'd filed the long form.

An amended return can make a lot of sense and result in a minor windfall for you. It's usually worth the time and effort it takes to file one. You pay the IRS plenty every year. Don't hesitate to ask for some of it back if you feel you have it coming to you.

Note: If you do file an amended federal return, you may also want to file an amended state return for the same year. Why? Because the IRS and your state revenue department are probably in close contact. The IRS will inform your state that you've amended your federal return. And if your amendment gets you a refund from the IRS, it might mean extra cash from your state, too.

Can You Be Audited Again—and Again?

A lot of taxpayers are worried about repeat audits. Relax. If you were audited last year, chances are you won't be this year.

Here's the way the system works: The IRS screens every individual return it receives for its audit potential. About two million out of the 90 million or so filed each year are red flagged. (That's a very small percentage.) Most of these are chosen because it looks as if they'll yield extra tax dollars. Others are picked purely at random.

If you had the unpleasant experience of being called in last year, think back to why the IRS questioned your return. Maybe your medical deductions were higher than average. Or maybe you made an honest mistake on your return. Or maybe you did something else out of the ordinary that set off the IRS's computer. In any case, you probably proved whatever you needed to prove, and that was that.

Depending on the problem you had then, it is possible (but not likely) that your return will be singled out again this year. An auditor may want to see if you're handling things properly this time around.

You've undoubtedly heard stories about taxpayers who have been audited again and again. If for some reason this has happened to you, then you know how expensive, time-consuming, and aggravating it can be.

What if the IRS comes after you this year, too? Well, *if* you've been audited repeatedly, *and* if you've always been audited on the same types of items, *and* if the IRS has never found anything wrong with your return, you can tell them to *cut it out.*

Write them a polite letter or call them and explain the situation. Remind them that they've never assessed you any back taxes. End by saying that, under the circumstances, you don't want to be audited again.

The IRS will check out your story. If everything is in order, they may actually call off this year's audit. They don't have to—but they might.

Be Aggressive yet Reasonable When Claiming Your Deductions

It's no secret that the IRS's computers are biased. They're programmed to locate errors on taxpayers' returns that hurt the IRS. However, they don't usually identify errors that hurt taxpayers—errors people make because they're too conservative with their returns. It's up to you to claim each and every tax deduction the law allows. If you miss one, the IRS isn't about to remind you to take it.

But what about the so-called "gray areas"—deductions that aren't cut-and-dried as far as the tax law is concerned? Should you decide these in your favor, or the IRS's?

The question most taxpayers ask themselves when they're faced with this decision is, "Will taking a particular deduction get me audited?" Often the answer depends on what tax professionals term the "audit lottery." You may be surprised to learn that the odds of your winning this lottery—that is, of *not* being audited—are pretty good.

Here are the facts:

1. Fewer than 2 percent of all returns filed by taxpayers in the lower income brackets are selected for audit.

2. Only about 8 percent of the returns filed by taxpayers earning more than $50,000 are audited, and 40 percent of these audits result in little or no change in the amount of taxes owed.

In other words, *nine out of ten* taxpayers in relatively high income brackets are not audited. And of those who are, only 60 percent end up owing more taxes.

This doesn't mean that you should feel free to cheat on your return. What it does mean is that you should be more comfortable with deciding gray areas in your favor.

Example: You want to deduct a casualty loss rather than file a claim with your insurance company that's almost guaranteed to boost your rates. The IRS says that you can't deduct this loss unless you first file a claim and get turned down. The Tax Court, on the other hand, tends to rule in the taxpayer's favor when they decide this issue.

If you decide to skip this deduction, the IRS will probably process your return, no questions asked. And you'll lose the tax break.

But if you choose to take this deduction—and, according to the Tax Court, you're entitled to it—the IRS may audit you, deny this deduction, and bill you for more taxes.

What's the bottom line? If you *don't* claim the casualty

loss, you *won't* get the tax break. If you *do* claim it, you *may* get it.

You'll feel better about taking this deduction if you figure out ahead of time the worst that can happen to you if the IRS selects your return for audit. How can you do this? By preparing *two* tax returns.

On the first, decide each and every questionable item in the IRS's favor. If you can't prove a particular deduction, don't take it.

On the second, decide all of the gray areas in your favor. Take every deduction or credit the law allows, even the shakiest ones.

Then figure the difference between the final numbers on each return. This will be your tax liability *if:*

1. the IRS audits your return;

2. they challenge every gray area on it; *and*

3. they turn down your interpretation of each one.

What's the likelihood that all of this will happen? Very remote. But even if it does, you'll at least know how much (if any) damage the IRS can inflict on you.

Which of the two returns should you actually file? Neither. Instead, make up a third return—and compromise a bit. Be aggressive, but be reasonable. Take the questionable deductions you're most sure of, and give a few to the IRS. That way you won't set off all the bells and whistles on their computer—and you'll stand a better chance of coming out ahead.

Good News about Your 1978 and 1979 Returns

Relax! Chances are the IRS isn't going to question your 1978 return. And your 1979 return is probably okay, too.

As a general rule, the IRS has up to three years from the April 15 due date to audit individual tax returns. (If a return is filed after the normal deadline, the IRS has three years from the actual filing date.) This means that the IRS has until April 15, 1982, to audit the 1978 return you filed in 1979. However, for all intents and purposes, the IRS is no longer interested in it. They're not going to audit it—not in the few days remaining before the three-year statute of limitations runs out.

After this April, in other words, you can get rid of most of the records that support your 1978 return. Just be sure to keep a copy of the return itself, along with your W-2 forms and any other documents pertaining to your income. Also hold on to records dealing with the purchases and sales of property, stocks, houses, and other investments, since they will definitely have an effect on later years' returns.

Your 1979 return will soon be safe from audit, too. That's because the IRS has an internal operating rule stating that they will not only begin but also complete the audit of a personal individual income tax return within 26 months of its due date. According to this rule, all audits of 1979 returns (filed by April 15, 1980) will be started and finished no later than June 15, 1982. That doesn't give the IRS much time. If you haven't heard about your 1979 return by March, you probably won't.

The IRS is only now getting into auditing 1980 returns. Your 1981 return won't be audited for another year at the earliest, if at all. But it will remain available for audit until April 15, 1985, so do keep all of your supporting records until then.

There are two very important exceptions to the 26-month rule:

1. If the IRS decides to audit your 1980 return, you can bet they'll want to review your 1979 return, too.

2. The three-year statute of limitations doesn't apply to taxpayers who never filed a return in the first place. Nor does it apply to those who failed to report large amounts of their income—say, 26 percent or more. In cases like these, the IRS can ask to see returns and records dating back many years.

How to Guarantee an Audit

Some people will do anything to avoid paying all or part of their taxes. They're very creative when it comes to concocting elaborate schemes and excuses.

The IRS is notorious for not having a sense of humor. They

call these people illegal tax protesters, and they're cracking down on them more and more frequently. The IRS has said that they will pursue an illegal tax protester for as little as $25 in unpaid taxes.

If you get yourself properly—or mistakenly—identified as an illegal tax protester, you're sure to be audited. No two ways about it.

There are several particularly blatant schemes that the IRS picks up on right away. If you want to guarantee yourself an audit, try any of the following:

1. Form a phony religious organization with your family and friends.

This is rapidly becoming the most popular of all tax protest devices. A group of taxpayers decides to band together and call themselves a tax-exempt church. Then they contribute up to 50 percent of their income (the most allowed in any one year) to their "church," substantially reducing their personal tax liability.

Some even take a vow of poverty and give 100 percent of their income to their "church," which in turn pays all of their expenses. At tax time, they claim that as ministers under a vow of poverty they aren't required to pay taxes.

The IRS recognizes the many legitimate ministers who file returns and honestly report the income they're supposed to. But because of the numerous church-related schemes around these days, examiners are on the lookout for suspicious returns.

2. File a fraudulent W-4.

The number of exemptions you claim on your W-4 determines how much money is withheld from your paychecks for taxes. Some protesters claim so many exemptions that they end up with no withholding. Usually they don't even bother to file returns.

If you're entitled to several exemptions, you should go ahead and take them. Just be aware that your employer is required to tell the IRS if you claim more than nine (a number that may soon go up to 14). And since the IRS is trying to cut down on false W-4s, they'll probably ask you to verify your exemptions.

3. Claim that paying taxes violates your constitutional rights.

Some taxpayers deliberately misinterpret the Constitution in an attempt to get out of paying their taxes. For example, they read the fourth amendment—the one dealing with "unreasonable searches and seizures"—and decide that the IRS has no right to "seize" their money. Or they use the eighth amendment—the one about "excessive fines" and "cruel and unusual punishment"—and come to the same conclusion. Or they insist that their right to privacy means that they don't have to answer the questions on their returns.

By all means, familiarize yourself with the Constitution. Just don't use it to avoid paying your taxes. The U. S. Supreme Court has consistently denied claims of this type.

4. Claim that since U.S. Federal Reserve Notes aren't redeemable in gold or silver, they have no value and therefore don't count as income.

As an alternative to this gold or silver standard scheme, you can argue that the dollar is declining so rapidly that it's worthless.

5. Refuse to pay your taxes because you don't approve of where your tax money goes.

Some protesters are opposed to defense spending or other government programs. To them, paying taxes is the same as supporting these programs. The IRS wants their money anyway.

These five schemes are simply the most common ones. There are others that tax protesters use regularly. None of them work.

If you don't believe this, try pulling one yourself. The IRS will identify you as a possible illegal tax protester and notify you that your return has been selected for audit.

VII.

DEALING WITH THE IRS

The IRS is like no other government agency. They have tremendous powers. However, this doesn't mean that you can't or shouldn't work with them to resolve disputes that arise from time to time.

They have a system, and in most cases it's effective. You may doubt this, especially if you've ever run head-on into their bureaucracy, but it's true. If you work within their system, you can usually come up with a reasonable solution to your problem, save yourself some tax dollars, and steer clear of potentially dangerous situations.

The key, of course, is to behave in a professional, businesslike manner—and remain calm!

Never Ignore the IRS

Even the IRS makes mistakes sometimes. Unfortunately, their mistakes can cost you money. That's why you should never, *ever* ignore their letters or notices—even when they're wrong.

Example: You file your tax return and claim a $500 refund. A few months go by and you get a letter from your IRS Service Center, informing you that you don't have a refund coming after all. Instead, it seems that they found out about some unreported income listed under your social security number, and you owe an additional $300 in back taxes.

You check your records and discover that the IRS made an error. They must have gotten you mixed up with some other taxpayer, because the unreported income wasn't yours.

What should you do? Write the IRS back *immediately* and explain the problem. *Don't ignore their letter.* When faced with a situation like this, some people think, "The IRS goofed—not me. Why should I take the trouble to answer them?" If you take this attitude, you may find the IRS knocking at your door someday.

You could find that the IRS has gone to your bank and taken the $300 they claim you owe out of your account. Your wages could be attached and your credit rating ruined. Your automobile could be seized. All because you didn't respond to their letter. The IRS isn't shy about going after taxpayers they feel are being uncooperative.

What if the IRS is right and you're wrong? Send them a check as soon as you can. If you don't have the money available, at least call or write them and try to work something out. You'll want to do this before they turn to their collection division. Once they reach that point, they can be very uncompromising.

My advice is to *always* answer *any* correspondence you receive from the IRS. Unless your file has been lost or misplaced in the bureaucratic red tape (this doesn't happen very often), you should hear from them fairly soon. Chances are that the problem or misunderstanding between you can be solved easily and quickly. Just don't put off responding, or things may get out of hand.

Bearing the Burden of Proof

When it comes to taxes and the IRS, there are a lot of myths floating around. This may be the most common one:

"If the IRS thinks I've done something wrong, that's their problem. They can't prove it!"

The fact is that unless you're accused of fraud or some other criminal activity related to your taxes, the IRS doesn't have to prove a thing. The burden of proof is on you—the taxpayer.

Example: You tossed a $20 bill into your church collection plate last Christmas. You include it in the charitable contributions deduction on your 1981 return.

If the IRS decides to audit your return, and the auditor asks about the $20, you may end up not being able to claim it. Why? Because you don't have a receipt or cancelled check to back it up.

This doesn't necessarily mean that the auditor *will* turn down this part of your deduction. If you're generally believable, he or she may allow it even without proof. Auditors are permitted to exercise some discretion.

Here's another popular myth:

"If you can't prove a deduction, you can't claim it."

Wrong! If you donated a box of clothing to the Salvation Army or Goodwill, go ahead and place a reasonable value on it. If you drove your car on business last year but didn't keep careful records, take your mileage and estimate as best you can the amount of gasoline you used and the cost of any repairs you had made.

Just keep in mind that the burden of proving each and every item on your return may fall on your shoulders if the IRS should decide to question you. How can you make this a little easier on yourself? By setting up your records so you don't fall into any tax traps.

There are three things you may have to prove if you're ever called in for an audit:

1. You may have to verify that you filed your return, and that you filed it on time.

The best way to avoid any problem in this area is to hand-deliver your return to the IRS District Office. Not many people want to take the trouble to do this, though. A more realistic approach is to send your return to the IRS Service Center by certified mail, return receipt requested. (The cost of the postage is tax deductible.) And do it by April 15.

Keep a copy of your return for your files, along with a note specifying the date on which you sent the original to the IRS.

2. You may have to prove that the income you reported is really what you earned.

Few people have trouble proving their salary and wages.

Dividend income and interest income are usually fairly straight-forward, too. If you have other sources of income as well, though, watch out.

You can get into trouble if the IRS tries to reconstruct your income through your bank records. Can you accurately identify each and every deposit you made during the past two or three years? Probably not. Under the tax law, the IRS can label all unidentified deposits as "income."

My advice is to make a note in your checkbook register beside each deposit you make from now on. For example: "salary," "dividend from AT&T," "interest from Dominion Bank." Mark all non-income items as such and give a brief explanation. For example: "transfer from savings account at credit union," "gift from Aunt Harriet," "repayment of loan to son-in-law." By keeping careful notes and records, you will have the answers if the IRS ever asks about your deposits.

3. You may have to prove all of your deductions.

This can be tough if you don't have receipts or cancelled checks for everything. The tax rules are especially strict when it comes to travel and entertainment expenses.

Don't let this stop you from deducting expenses you actually incurred. Unless the IRS calls you in for an audit, you won't have to verify exact amounts. And sometimes other types of records can be helpful.

Example: You took a client to lunch last February, paid cash, and forgot to pick up the receipt. You do have a stub from the garage where you parked your car, though.

Should you estimate what you paid for the business lunch and take it as a business expense? Yes. If you're audited in the future, you won't be able to prove the exact amount you spent on lunch, but that may not be necessary. You'll have the stub from the parking garage, and that will help. If you also remembered to put a note in your calendar about the lunch date, the IRS will be even more likely to believe you.

Who's Responsible for a Joint Return?

Financial affairs are a family matter. At tax time, husband and wife alike should be involved in filling out the forms. Both should go through all of the numbers on the return—together. And both should review the supporting records and receipts. There's no reason why each partner shouldn't know everything there is to know about the family's taxes.

And there are a lot of reasons why both partners *should* be fully informed. Unexpected things happen. Couples separate and get divorced. People die.

The IRS believes that each person who signs a joint return is responsible for it. The *whole* return—not just half. If you and your spouse file jointly, for example, and the IRS decides to audit your return, they'll usually ask both of you to come in.

What if your partner isn't available? Then the burden of defending the joint return will fall on you alone. If as a result of the audit the IRS wants more money, they won't care which one of you pays it. They'll go after whoever is easiest to find and collect from.

Fortunately for some people, the tax law does make allowances for an "innocent spouse"—a person whose partner was negligent or downright dishonest when it came to filling out the joint return. If you're audited and the IRS slaps you with a bill for more taxes, penalties, interest, and so forth, you *may* be able to get off the hook, but only if:

1. you filed a joint return with your spouse for the year in question; *and*

2. your spouse failed to report at least 25 percent of his or her income; *and*

3. you had no idea that the money wasn't reported, and had no reason to know about the money; *and*

4. it really doesn't seem fair to hold you responsible for the tax problem.

Who decides the fairness issue? The IRS. They'll do their best to find out whether or not you might have significantly benefited from the income you supposedly didn't know about. It may be tough for you to prove that you didn't.

In other words, it's very difficult to come under the protection of the "innocent spouse" rule. It can be done, but only under the most extreme circumstances.

That's why it's so important for you to take an active role in your family's financial and tax affairs. Once you sign your name to a joint return, it becomes your responsibility. The IRS rarely accepts excuses of any kind.

Make Sure That Your Check to the IRS Is Good

It can be embarrassing to bounce a check. When dealing with the IRS, it can be downright expensive.

Let's say you prepare your return and end up owing the IRS. You write them a check, stick it in the envelope along with your return, and mail it off to the Service Center by April 15.

That's the end of it for another year, right?

Not necessarily.

Under the tax law, the IRS doesn't consider your taxes paid until your check (or money order) clears. If for some reason it doesn't, you could be in trouble.

You'll immediately be liable for the same penalties and interest charges you'd have to pay if you never sent your check in the first place. The IRS will also slap you with another penalty—a minimum of $5, or a maximum of 1 percent of the amount of your check over $500, whichever is greater—just for bouncing your check. This penalty can in some cases be forgiven, *if* you had a good reason to believe that your check was covered when you mailed it, and *if* you can prove it.

Example: An unwary taxpayer—let's call him Ernie—participated in a money market mutual fund that paid high (market rate) interest. He had a very good year—so good, in fact, that he owed the IRS $15,000.

On April 8, seven days before the filing deadline, Ernie made a large deposit into his money market account, anticipating his tax bill. On April 15, he filed for an automatic 60-day extension and sent the IRS a draft for $15,000 drawn on his money fund.

Two weeks later, Ernie learned that the fund had bounced his draft. Not for "insufficient funds"—Ernie had put plenty of money into his account ahead of time—but for "uncollected funds."

The place where Ernie had his money market fund required a deposit to sit in an account for at least 15 business days before any of it could be withdrawn. The IRS tried to cash Ernie's draft as soon as they received it. His seven-day-in-advance deposit hadn't been made soon enough.

What happened to Ernie? A lot.

First, the IRS turned down his request for an extension, since they hadn't been able to collect on his draft. And they charged Ernie a 5 percent per month late filing penalty.

In addition, Ernie had to pay a one-half of 1 percent per month late payment penalty for every month that passed until he mailed the IRS a new—good—draft.

Finally, he had to pay interest on the amount he owed and, of course, the 1 percent fee for bouncing his check. (That fee alone amounted to $150.)

All because of a timing error.

The message is clear: Do *not* bounce a tax payment check. Here are a few guidelines you can use to prevent this sort of thing from happening to you:

1. Before you write a check to the IRS, be sure that there's enough money in your account to cover it.

2. Don't play the float game. The IRS has a policy of immediately cashing all checks it receives. So you can't expect much of a delay between the time you mail your check and the time the IRS presents it for payment. At most, you'll have a few days.

3. If you're writing a draft on a money market fund or some other investment account, be aware that financial institutions often impose clearing time requirements. Your bank, savings and loan, or credit union might hold on to your money for a similar grace period, even if it's in an ordinary checking account.

The IRS Must Pay You Interest—Sometimes

Believe it or not, there are times when the IRS is required to send interest payments to taxpayers. According to IRS estimates, they'll be mailing out a total of $600 million during this year alone.

If any of it comes your way, you'll have to declare it as

income and pay tax on it. You can count on the IRS to send a Form 1099 to you *and* their computers reporting this interest income.

Here's the key: The IRS has 45 days from the date when you file your return, or its due date (whichever is later), to mail you your refund. If they're late, they have to pay you interest on the amount they owe.

If you file your return on April 15, in other words, and you claim a refund, the IRS must mail it to you by June 1 or pay you interest. However, if you file in January, February, or March, the IRS still has until June 1 because the due date of your return is April 15. If for some reason you wait until June 15 to mail your refund claim, the IRS has until July 30 to send you your refund.

But this isn't the only instance in which the IRS must pay interest to taxpayers.

Example: The IRS calls you in to audit your 1980 tax return (which you filed on time last year). Instead of you owing them more money, though, it turns out that you have an additional refund coming. The IRS must then send you a check covering not only the amount of the refund but also any interest that accrues between June 1, 1981 (45 days past your 1980 return's due date) and when they finally settle up with you.

Example: You learn of a tax break that you've previously overlooked. You decide to file an amended return. *If* the IRS accepts your refund claim, they'll send you your additional refund plus interest.

Example: You suffer tax losses that can be carried back and applied to earlier returns. Because this will effectively cut your tax bills for those years, the IRS will have to send you a refund plus interest.

There are also appeal actions you can take that may result in refunds and additional interest.

Whether the IRS owes you interest on a particular return —and exactly how much—depends on when you originally filed it.

The annual interest rate has varied over the years. Between February 1, 1980 and January 31, 1982, it was 12 percent. Before that it was 7 percent. From February 1,

1982 through December 31, 1982, the rate will be a whopping 20 percent, thanks to the Economic Recovery Tax Act of 1981.

Let an IRS PRO Help You with Your Tax Problem

There is a way to cut through IRS red tape—if you know where to call and who to ask for.

The IRS offers a service called the Problem Resolution Program. Their Problem Resolution Officers (PROs) are specially trained to help taxpayers through sticky situations. During one recent 12-month period, IRS PROs handled 400,000 taxpayer complaints. Here's a list of the most common ones:

- Refund not received (13.9% of all inquiries were in this area)
- No response from the IRS Service Center to a specific question (9.9%)
- Refund check lost or stolen (6.4%)
- Problem with claim/amended return (6.3%)
- Unclear computer notice from the IRS Service Center (5.6%)
- Problem with invalid or duplicate social security number (5.2%)
- Problem with error processing at the IRS (4.7%)
- Taxpayer misunderstanding (4.5%)
- Problem with the IRS collection process (4.4%)

PROs handle other red-tape situations, too.

Example: You receive a notice (Form CP 2000) from the IRS. That's a letter stating that the income you reported in your tax return differed from the information furnished to the IRS by a company that paid you interest, dividends, etc. You look back through your documents and discover that one of the payer-furnished reports the IRS received about you was wrong. It's up to *you* to prove it—and convince the IRS computer that you don't owe the extra tax they're asking for.

The first thing you should do is answer the IRS's letter. Explain the situation in writing as clearly as you can. If this doesn't work, call your local IRS office and talk to someone there.

If it becomes obvious that the usual IRS problem-solving procedures aren't working for you, ask to speak to a PRO. He or she will be able to give you the most help in the shortest period of time.

In fact, you should contact a PRO for any non-audit problem that can't be resolved after one or two letters or phone calls. (Do not ask a PRO to help you through an audit or even advise you on it. That's not their job.) If your problem can't be solved within five working days, the PRO will get back to you, bring you up to date, and tell you how soon he or she expects to have your case settled.

I know for a fact that some IRS officers try to discourage taxpayers from asking PROs for help. If everybody knew about this program, they feel, then too many people would sidestep normal IRS procedures. If you sense that you're being put off, don't give up. Keep asking for a PRO until you get one.

VIII.
DEVELOPING A YEAR-ROUND TAX PLAN

Long-range tax planning is the only, repeat only, way to reduce your annual tax bill to its lowest possible legal limit. If you're serious about saving money, you can't wait until November or December to start thinking about your taxes. That's just too late.

You should formulate a tax strategy that's right for you and follow it all 12 months of the year. Update and revise it constantly. Consult it whenever you're considering making an investment or changing your financial situation in any way. Never make a money decision without first determining its tax effects.

You *can* take control of your own financial affairs. It's not that hard to do. You'll probably need to break some old, bad habits—but you'll be glad you did when April 15 rolls around.

Analyzing Past Years' Returns

It's almost impossible to make tax plans for the future without first analyzing the past. If you want to determine where you should go, you should start by finding out where you've been.

Pull out copies of your last three or four years' tax returns.

On a separate piece of paper, list all of the income items that apply to you—salary, interest, dividends, capital gains and losses, state income tax refunds, pensions, annuities, rental income, royalties, self-employment income, and so on. Do the same for your deductions and credits. Then list the taxes you paid and refunds you received.

Make up a chart with columns for these various categories and for each year you want to examine. Your chart might look like the one shown here.

Category	Year			
	1977	1978	1979	1980
INCOME				
Salary				
Interest				
Dividends				
State tax refunds				
Rental income				
Capital gains				
Other				
TOTAL				
ADJUSTMENTS TO INCOME				
Moving expenses				
Alimony paid				
IRA or Keogh plan				
Other				
TOTAL				
ITEMIZED DEDUCTIONS				
Medical				
Taxes paid				
State withholding				
Interest paid				
Mortgage				
Charitable contributions (cash)				
Charitable contributions (noncash)				
Casualty losses				
Tax preparation fees				

Category		Year		
	1977	1978	1979	1980
ITEMIZED DEDUCTIONS (Continued) Job hunting expenses				
Other				
TOTAL				
TAX CREDITS Residential energy				
Political contributions				
Child and dependent care				
Other				
TOTAL				
TOTAL TAX LIABILITY				
TAX PAYMENTS Federal withholding				
Quarterly estimated payments				
REFUNDS				

Now fill in the figures from each year's tax return. Spend some time looking them over. Compare them to one another. Make footnotes at the bottom of your chart to explain some of the differences. Did you get a large increase in salary two years ago when you changed jobs? Did your deductions take a big jump when you bought your new house? When, if ever, did you use income averaging to lower your taxes?

On a new sheet of paper, write down what tax moves—if any—you made at the end of each year. Did you ever speed up your deductions and delay your income to cut your tax bill? Did you sell any securities at the last minute or buy into some tax shelter investments?

When you've finished with your chart and your notes, you'll have a complete history of your taxes for the past three or four years. You'll be able to tell at a glance which years' taxes had special quirks, which of your tax plans worked (and which didn't), and almost anything else you want to know.

Armed with this information, you can start thinking about the tax-reducing moves and techniques that are available to you this year.

Make up a chart every year from now on. Keep old charts for future reference. You'll be amazed at how much they help.

How to Get Copies of Your Old Returns

Your permanent files should include copies of your income tax returns from several years back. They contain numbers you may need for tax planning reasons, both now and in the future.

For example, an old tax return will help you as you compute the gain on the sale of your home. You'll also have to consult past returns if you ever decide to income average or file an amended return to correct an earlier oversight or error.

If you haven't kept copies of your returns, contact your local IRS office. Ask them to send you Form 4506, Request for Copy of Tax Return. (You'll need a separate form for each return you want the IRS to find for you.) On it you'll be asked to identify the type of return you filed (personal, employment, gift tax, etc.), the year for which you filed it, and so on.

Then send it to whichever IRS Service Center you *originally* filed the return with.

Example: You lived in Virginia for a while and filed your 1977 return at the IRS Service Center in Memphis, Tennessee. You've since moved to Arizona, and you now mail your returns to the Service Center in Ogden, Utah. In order to get a copy of your 1977 return, you'll have to send your Form 4506 to Memphis.

The IRS will mail you copies of any returns you ask for, and they'll only charge you a small fee—a couple dollars each.

Caution: If you need a copy of a missing return in order to compute your 1981 taxes, you have a problem. Typically, the IRS takes six weeks or more to search their records, make copies, and get them to you. During tax filing season, it takes even longer. Don't count on receiving your copies in time.

Mail your Form 4506 anyway and do one of two things:

1. Complete your 1981 return to the best of your ability and file it by April 15. When the copy of your old return arrives, file an amended return if necessary. Or:

2. File for an automatic extension (Form 4868). That gives you 60 extra days in which to file your return. Within those eight weeks, you *may* get the copy you need.

Recommendation: If you've been using the same tax preparer for years, check first with him or her. Many preparers keep copies of the returns they do for their clients.

Record Keeping

Careful record keeping is an essential part of any good tax strategy. Your long-range plans may be brilliant, but without thorough records you won't stand a chance if the IRS ever decides to audit you. The fact is that the IRS seldom denies deductions and credits to people who can back them up with documentation.

Under the tax law, it's your responsibility to verify any and all items the IRS questions. What if you can't prove a particular deduction? If push comes to shove, the IRS probably won't allow it. And if you make a habit of keeping sloppy records (or no records at all), you may end up in big trouble.

Your record keeping system does *not* have to be elaborate. A series of file folders (or even large envelopes) labeled "Income," "House Expenses," "Investments," "Medical Expenses," "Automobile Expenses," and so forth is usually sufficient. For convenience, arrange the folders alphabetically and store them in a handy drawer at home.

Once a week, gather together all of the chits and receipts you've accumulated during the past several days and put them into the proper files. Write directly on each slip the date of the transaction, the amount, the purpose, and any and all other information that could help you to verify a future tax claim. Keep running totals for the contents of every file.

Make sure that your pocket or desk calendar is always up-to-date. Use it to record business luncheons, mileage, out-of-town trips, and any other meetings or appointments that could lead to tax deductions.

The more records you have, the more claims you'll be able to prove—and the more money you'll save. There's no such thing as being too prepared.

Good record keeping offers another plus: You'll be constantly aware of your tax position. As a result, you'll have a better handle on which financial moves will affect your taxes and which won't. And that's what tax planning is all about.

Prepare Mock Returns at Different Times during the Year

Your yearly tax situation is something you should think about *at least* once every three months. My advice is to set up four separate tax planning and reviewing sessions during the year. Here's a suggested schedule:

Session I.

This should take place during the filing season. If you start working on your 1981 return in March, 1982, that's when you should also begin considering tax cutting moves and strategies for your 1982 return.

Session II.

Plan this for June or early July. With the year half over, you should be able to get a fairly accurate idea of what your 1982 earnings, deductions, credits, and withholding will be. Take a look at what's happening with your stocks and other investments, and try to project what's likely to happen during the next few months.

Session III.

This should take place in September. With the year drawing to a close, it will be time to start putting some of your tax plans into action. Then you won't be rushed at year-end into making last-minute moves that work against you rather than for you.

Session IV.

Take the long Thanksgiving weekend—or some other weekend during November—to finalize your tax plans for the year.

What should you do during each session? Start by computing your year-to-date income, deductions, credits, and withholding. Don't forget any quarterly estimated tax payments you've already made. Anticipate how these same items will look by the end of the year. Using these figures, prepare a mock return that reflects how you think your taxes will look at filing time.

Compare each mock return with the real ones you filed during the past three or four years. Then ask yourself as many questions as you can come up with. Will you be paying more, or less, in taxes this year than in previous years? Will you end up overpaying the IRS? Are you forgetting to take deductions you're entitled to?

Finally, write down what financial events you think will occur before your next tax planning session. List any particulars. Will you be making a securities sale? Selling your house? Getting married or divorced? Is there anything at all you're about to do that will affect this year's taxes?

By examining your tax situation four times a year, you'll always know where you stand. You'll be able to tell well in advance of the April 15 filing date whether you're going to owe the IRS—and, if so, how much—or if you'll be claiming a refund. You'll know when your tax plans aren't working and when they are.

How to Tell Whether a Tax Move
Will Fit into Your Plan

Before you make any tax move, you should consider its effects very carefully. This is especially important during the last two or three months of the year, when you're doing your best to cut your tax bill down to its lowest legal limit. It's easy to do something rash when you're faced with a time crunch.

Some people go to the trouble of comparing "equivalent interest rates," "marginal tax brackets," and the like. But there's a much simpler—and far less confusing—way to determine the value of a particular tax strategy: Translate it into a dollar figure.

Example: Beginning in 1982, everyone who works is eligible to establish and fund an IRA (Individual Retirement

Account) with a maximum contribution of $2,000 or 100 percent of his or her income, whichever is lower.

You're single, and you expect to earn $30,000 during 1982. Based on your 1981 itemized deductions, you anticipate that you'll be deducting $5,000 for 1982, plus your $1,000 personal exemption, resulting in taxable income of $24,000. According to the IRS's rate schedules, you'll owe $5,012 in income taxes for the year.

What will happen if you decide to invest in an IRA? You'll be able to deduct an additional $2,000 and lower your taxable income to $22,000. Your final tax bill will then be $4,372. That's a $640 difference.

With these figures in front of you, you can make a sensible decision about whether or not to fund an IRA for 1982.

On the one hand, you'll be out the $2,000 until you reach age 59½. On the other, you'll be putting money away for your retirement. And you'll be reducing your 1982 tax bill by about $53 a month.

Each time you weigh a tax decision, sit down with a pencil and a piece of paper. Compute what your taxes will be if you take the action and if you don't. The difference between the two sets of figures will be your tax benefit.

When you've come up with bottom-line numbers—and not before—you'll be able to determine whether the tax move you have in mind will be worth the effort and money it may cost you.

Break the Overwithholding Habit

Seventy-five to 80 percent of all individual taxpayers send in returns calling for refunds. In 1981, the average refund came to $634. Over the years, the trend has been for still more taxpayers to file for increasingly larger refunds.

Although it may feel good to get that annual check from the IRS, there are three reasons why you should break the overwithholding/refund habit:

1. It's up to the Postal Service to handle your refund in a timely manner. If your check is lost in the mail or returned to the IRS, you could spend months or longer trying to get it sent back to you or reprocessed.

2. You'll become a much better taxpayer if you start breaking even with the IRS or *owing* a bit (within a hundred dollars) at year-end. This is because most people who are expecting refunds generally avoid the gray areas on their returns. They don't want to do anything that might call attention to themselves or delay their refund checks.

Here's an example of this type of thinking: "Why should I take a $200 deduction for employee business expenses, even though I'm legally entitled to it? If I do, I may get audited."

Nonsense! Take the deductions you're entitled to—all of them.

I've found that those taxpayers who owe the IRS money will dig for everything they're able to get. They're much more aggressive with their returns than people who have refunds coming.

3. Taxpayers who are asking for refunds tend to file earlier than those who aren't. They want their money back as soon as possible. I've found that people who prepare their returns early and then *review* them after some weeks have passed frequently find more items to claim. In general, those who file early don't review their returns to see whether they've missed anything.

How can you break (or at least cut down on) your withholding/refund habit? It's easy. Just keep close track of your income and deductions during the year. *And adjust your Form W-4,* Employee Withholding Certificate. This is the form that tells your employer how many exemptions you're claiming and, in effect, how much should be withheld from your paycheck in federal income tax.

Follow this rule of thumb: Claim "1" for each member of your family, another "1" if there's only one wage earner, *plus* additional exemptions for what are called "excess itemized deductions."

Example: A married person with one child and large itemized deductions due to high mortgage payments (interest and real estate taxes) may be able to claim *eight or nine* exemptions on his or her W-4.

There's been a lot of talk about fraudulent withholding forms, and I'm certainly not suggesting that you get involved in anything like that. But if you're entitled to a large number of exemptions, take them and stop overwithholding.

You should know that your employer is required to notify the IRS if you claim more than nine exemptions. (This number may soon increase to 14.) However, if you're entitled to as many as 15 or 20—and I know some people who are—go ahead and take them. The IRS may ask why you're claiming so many, but as long as they're legal you shouldn't have any problem.

My advice is to ask your employer to give you a blank W-4 form. Read the instructions on it and determine how many exemptions you can legitimately claim to end your overwithholding/refund habit.

Shifting Your Income and Deductions

There's a time-honored and perfectly reasonable way to reduce your income tax liability during any given year: Speed up your deductions and credits so you can take them during the current year, and deflect some of your income into the following year.

A lot of people know about this strategy, but not enough bother to put it into action. Can it work for you? That depends on your own tax situation.

Start by considering your deductions and credits. Under the tax law, if you pay for a tax-deductible item before the end of the year, you can claim it on that year's return.

This means that every September or October you should take a long, hard look at any outstanding bills you have and any purchases or charitable donations you're thinking of making.

What about the amount due for your son's orthodontic work? Do you need a new pair of glasses? Do you live in an older home, and are you planning to add some insulation and storm windows that will qualify for the residential energy tax credit? Does your garage need cleaning out—and can you donate some of your usable items to a worthwhile organization? How about giving your old gas-guzzler to your local high school auto shop? Or passing some books along to your library?

If you attend school and your expenses qualify for the educational expense deduction, you may want to pay your winter semester's tuition by year-end. Buy your books early, too. Pay your personal property taxes in December rather than waiting until January. If you're going to owe additional state and/or local taxes for the year, send in your check by December 31.

Any and all of these moves can boost your deductions. But what if you don't have enough ready cash on hand? That's a problem many taxpayers face.

You have two options that may never have occurred to you: You can take out a short-term loan, or you can use a credit card to make payments on tax-deductible items. Any interest you pay on the loan—or the charge—is eventually deductible. What if you don't pay off your credit card company until the following year? That won't matter to the IRS. They'll let you take the deduction for the year in which you charged your payment.

Accelerating deductions is an easy way to cut your tax bill. Deflecting income is a bit more difficult, but it can be done.

Caution: You can't postpone some types of income. If you don't pick up your December 28 salary check until January 3, you'll still have to pay taxes on it as of December.

However, you may be able to delay a bonus or a commission. And you may be able to put off payments from people you do business with. Just don't send out your invoices for a week or two.

Now that you know some of the more common ways of shifting income and deductions between different tax years, it's up to you to decide whether or not you want to use this tax strategy. It often makes good sense, but not always.

How can you tell if it will work to your advantage? By sitting down and figuring it out on paper. Determine the dollars-and-cents value of a particular income or deduction shift. Find out the actual tax effect that such a move will have.

Try to forecast your next year's tax situation. Will it be better to save some deductions until then? Should you bill a client now instead of later?

Just because you're aware of a tax strategy doesn't necessarily mean you should use it. Take the time to determine whether it's right for you.

Year-End Gifts

Some people give away large amounts of money or property at the end of the year in an attempt to reduce their overall tax bills. What they often don't realize is that while some gifts are deductible, others aren't.

According to the tax law, gifts fall into two distinct categories:

1. donations of cash, property, investments, land, etc. to recognized charitable, educational, or religious organizations; and

2. gifts of money, property, etc. to family members.

The first type is tax deductible. (See Chapter III, "Deducting Charitable Contributions," "How To Deduct Noncash Donations to Charity," and "Not All Charitable Contributions Are Immediately Deductible.")

The second type is *not* tax deductible. You will realize a future tax *break* of sorts if you make year-end gifts to family members. However, giving away too much could result in a tax *liability* to you.

Here are the rules:

1. For 1981, you're allowed to give away as much as $3,000 in cash or property to as many people as you want before you get involved with the gift tax. If you give any one person more than $3,000, you'll have to report it. If there are four people you feel like being generous to, you can give each of them $3,000 for a grand total of $12,000.

A husband-wife team can jointly give away as much as $6,000 to as many people as they want, but they can't give any one person more than that amount without reporting it.

2. Beginning in 1982, the $3,000 per person per year limit is raised to $10,000, and the $6,000 husband-wife limit jumps to $20,000. Again, you can give away these amounts to as many people as you want. For tax purposes, you may not want to give any one person more than the limit.

Where's the tax break? Not on your income tax bill. The only income tax relief you'll get will come in future years, when you won't have to pay tax on the interest income the money would have earned if it had remained in your bank account.

Where's the tax liability? If you stay within the $3,000–$6,000 per person per year limits for 1981 (and the $10,000–$20,000 limits for 1982), there won't be any. But if you exceed them, you will have to *report* the gifts you make for gift tax purposes, although you may not have to actually pay gift taxes on them.

Is it worth it to make large year-end gifts? To charity—yes. To family members—maybe. You may want to shift some of the interest income burden off of yourself and on to someone else who's in a lower tax bracket.

Example: You give your son $1,000 in December, 1981. For 1982, you won't have to pay tax on the interest the money would have earned if you'd kept it in your own account. If your son banks the money, though, he'll have to start declaring the interest income on his tax return—if he's required to file. Depending on his income level, he may not have to file, and no one will have to pay taxes on the interest.

Savings Plans

As you're developing a tax strategy, be sure to consider your savings accounts, too. The amount of interest income you have to report (and pay taxes on) in any given year depends in part on the types of investments you make.

Example: In October, 1981, three single taxpayers and one married couple put $10,000 each into different savings plans.

Mildred went to her bank and purchased a six-month money-market certificate. She was given the choice of receiving monthly interest checks or waiting until her CD matured to collect the entire amount. She decided to take the monthly checks.

Douglas purchased a six-month CD at his savings and loan. But he opted for a "loophole" certificate—one that doesn't pay any interest until maturity.

Martha Ann bought a six-month Treasury Bill directly from the Bureau of the Public Debt. To get it, she had to call them on the telephone, ask for an application, fill it out, and mail them her $10,000 check.

Allie and Bernie, a married couple, bought an All Savers Certificate.

What are the tax effects of each savings plan?

Mildred has to report the three months' interest she received in 1981 on this year's tax return. The rest of the interest on her CD will be paid during 1982, and she'll report it on that year's return.

Douglas doesn't have any interest income from his CD to report on his 1981 return. He'll receive the full amount in early 1982, but he won't have to pay any taxes on it until April 15, 1983.

Within days after purchasing her Treasury Bill, Martha Ann received some money from the U.S. Government. According to the Treasury Department, their check to her isn't even termed an "interest" payment. Instead, it's an "original issue discount." It won't be considered taxable until 1982, when the security matures. Meanwhile Martha Ann can either spend the money or reinvest it—it's up to her. And she won't have to pay taxes on it until her 1982 return is due. Not bad.

Allie and Bernie aren't hurting, either. The interest they receive on their All Savers is tax-free, since they're filing jointly and the interest won't exceed $2,000 (the maximum they're allowed by law).

Weighing the Costs of Owing the IRS

Most people's tax bills are covered by withholding—money that's taken out of their paychecks. But some people are responsible for paying all or part of their own taxes.

If you're self-employed, the IRS expects you to make quarterly estimated tax payments. For each tax year, these are officially due on April 15, June 15, September 15, and the following January 15.

Even if your taxes are withheld for you, you may still have to make additional quarterly estimated payments. If you have a taxable pension or annuity, or if you realize a fairly large profit from the sale of assets like stocks or bonds, then you'll owe the IRS more taxes than your withholding allows for.

At tax time, you may discover that your withholding and/or quarterly payments more than took care of your tax bill. If this is the case, simply file your return and claim a refund.

But what if you end up owing a bit to the IRS? The obvious answer is to send them a check. There's a catch, though: Depending on how much you owe, the IRS may slap you with a stiff penalty for underpaying.

Here's what the tax law says:

1. If you owe the IRS additional taxes at the end of the year; *and*

2. if the amount you owe is greater than $100 (for 1981; this threshold increases to $200 for 1982); *and*

3. if your withholding and/or quarterly payments didn't cover at least 80 percent of your total tax liability; *then*

4. the IRS may be able to charge you an underpayment penalty.

This penalty is nondeductible—you won't be able to take it off of your next year's tax bill. Until January 31, 1982, the annual rate is 12 percent; after that it jumps to an all-time high of 20 percent.

You can avoid having to pay this penalty, but it will take some careful planning.

If you have supplementary income that isn't subject to withholding, you may want to increase the amount taken out of your paychecks. Get a new W-4 from your employer and start claiming fewer exemptions.

If you make quarterly estimated payments, send them in on time. With the help of a good tax plan, you should be able to sit down every three months or so and figure what you owe at that point with reasonable accuracy.

You may decide that it's better to keep underpaying the IRS. With the penalty at only 12 percent, some taxpayers would hold on to their tax money until the very last minute. Meanwhile, they would invest it at 16 to 20 percent. At tax time, they would send the IRS a check for whatever they owed, plus the 12 percent penalty, and still come out ahead.

With the 20 percent penalty rate, this may no longer be such a good strategy. Before you risk the penalty, make sure that it's worth it for you.

Getting Professional Help with Your Return

Income tax forms and instructions scare a lot of people. That's why so many taxpayers today hire professionals to handle their returns. Others hire tax preparers because their finances are complicated, or because they don't have enough time to do their own returns, or because they simply don't like dealing with all of the numbers and details involved.

Will *you* need professional help with your taxes this year? Not if you're comfortable handling your return and there haven't been any significant changes in your financial affairs during 1981. Why pay someone else to do what you're capable of doing yourself?

However, if you're reasonably sure that you won't be able to go it alone, start looking for help *now*. It's best to hire someone as early in the tax season as possible.

Should you look for a tax *advisor,* or a tax *preparer?* They're not necessarily one and the same. A tax *advisor* is someone who advises you about the tax effects of your financial deals and gives you assistance with tax planning. He or she may not even be in the business of preparing tax returns.

Use a tax advisor primarily for year-round tax planning. Find one around the middle of the year and work with him or her to develop a long-range tax strategy. Hiring one in January or later to work on your 1981 taxes won't make much sense, since there will be little advice he or she can give you that will make much difference on that return.

If you need help completing your 1981 return, find a tax *preparer.* This is someone who is familiar with all of the IRS's forms, has kept up-to-date on the changes in the tax law that have taken place over the past year, and is able to do your return in a competent and timely manner.

There are many differences among tax preparers, and fees vary. Commercial preparers do a thriving business during the January-April filing season and tend to be the least costly. You can expect to pay between $30-$60 to have your return prepared, *if* it's fairly basic.

Independent preparers are usually self-employed and may or may not be available year-round. A number of independents are ex-IRS employees.

Public accountants may be the best value as far as tax preparers go—if you can find one who specializes in taxes. Not all of them do.

Enrolled Agents are tax specialists who have passed a tough, IRS-administered examination. They usually know their taxes and are available throughout the year. Some of them now advertise in the Yellow Pages.

CPAs and tax attorneys tend to be expensive. If all you need is someone to prepare a relatively straightforward, personal income tax return, you may not require such high-powered help.

My advice is to find a tax preparer whose philosophy is similar to yours. If you're conservative, you won't want a tax rebel filling out your forms. On the other hand, you won't want someone who will let the IRS ride roughshod over your tax rights.

You should look for a fairly aggressive tax preparer who's in business all year long, not someone who folds up shop as soon as the filing season ends. If and when you do get called in for an audit, you'll want him or her to represent you. You may have to pay extra for this service.

Two red flags:

1. Watch out for a preparer who promises you that your return will definitely not be audited. No one can guarantee that, since the IRS chooses some returns for audit each year on a purely random basis. In addition, this type of preparer will probably fill out your return so conservatively that you'll end up overpaying your taxes.

2. Watch out for a preparer who promises you a refund *before* he or she has gone over all of your facts and figures.

Finally, keep in mind that you don't always get what you pay for when it comes to tax preparers. Never forget that, in the end, you're your own best financial advisor, and you should play an important role in the preparation of your tax return.

Appendix: Tax Rate Schedules

I. SINGLE TAXPAYERS

For Tax Year 1981

If taxable income is:	The tax is:
Not over $2,300	No tax
Over $2,300 but not over $3,400	14% of the amount over $2,300
Over $3,400 but not over $4,400	$154 + 16% of the amount over $3,400
Over $4,400 but not over $6,500	$314 + 18% of the amount over $4,400
Over $6,500 but not over $8,500	$692 + 14% of the amount over $6,500
Over $8,500 but not over $10,800	$1,072 + 21% of the amount over $8,500
Over $10,800 but not over $12,900	$1,555 + 24% of the amount over $10,800
Over $12,900 but not over $15,000	$2,059 + 26% of the amount over $12,900
Over $15,000 but not over $18,200	$2,605 + 30% of the amount over $15,000
Over $18,200 but not over $23,500	$3,565 + 34% of the amount over $18,200
Over $23,500 but not over $28,800	$5,367 + 39% of the amount over $23,500
Over $28,800 but not over $34,100	$7,434 + 44% of the amount over $38,800
Over $34,100 but not over $41,500	$9,766 + 49% of the amount over $34,100
Over $41,500 but not over $55,300	$13,392 + 55% of the amount over $41,500
Over $55,300 but not over $81,800	$20,982 + 63% of the amount over $55,300
Over $81,800 but not over $108,300	$37,677 + 68% of the amount over $81,800
Over $108,300	$55,697 + 70% of the amount over $108,300

For Tax Year 1982

If taxable income is:	The tax is:
Not over $2,300	No tax
Over $2,300 but not over $3,400	12% of the amount over $2,300
Over $3,400 but not over $4,400	$132 + 14% of the amount over $3,400
Over $4,400 but not over $6,500	$272 + 16% of the amount over $4,400
Over $6,500 but not over $8,500	$608 + 17% of the amount over $6,500
Over $8,500 but not over $10,800	$948 + 19% of the amount over $8,500
Over $10,800 but not over $12,900	$1,385 + 22% of the amount over $10,800
Over $12,900 but not over $15,000	$1,847 + 23% of the amount over $12,900
Over $15,000 but not over $18,200	$2,330 + 27% of the amount over $15,000
Over $18,200 but not over $23,500	$3,194 + 31% of the amount over $18,200
Over $23,500 but not over $28,800	$4,837 + 35% of the amount over $23,500
Over $28,800 but not over $34,100	$6,692 + 40% of the amount over $28,800
Over $34,100 but not over $41,500	$8,812 + 44% of the amount over $34,100
Over $41,500	$12,068 + 50% of the amount over $41,500

[148]

I. SINGLE TAXPAYERS *(continued)*

For Tax Year 1983

If taxable income is:	The tax is:
Not over $2,300	No tax
Over $2,300 but not over $3,400	11% of the amount over $2,300
Over $3,400 but not over $4,400	$121 + 13% of the amount over $3,400
Over $4,400 but not over $8,500	$251 + 15% of the amount over $4,400
Over $8,500 but not over $10,800	$866 + 17% of the amount over $8,500
Over $10,800 but not over $12,900	$1,257 + 19% of the amount over $10,800
Over $12,900 but not over $15,000	$1,656 + 21% of the amount over $12,900
Over $15,000 but not over $18,200	$2,097 + 24% of the amount over $15,000
Over $18,200 but not over $23,500	$2,865 + 28% of the amount over $18,200
Over $23,500 but not over $28,800	$4,349 + 32% of the amount over $23,500
Over $28,800 but not over $34,100	$6,045 + 36% of the amount over $28,800
Over $34,100 but not over $41,500	$7,953 + 40% of the amount over $34,100
Over $41,500 but not over $55,300	$10,913 + 45% of the amount over $41,500
Over $55,300	$17,123 + 50% of the amount over $55,300

For Tax Years After 1983

If taxable income is:	The tax is:
Not over $2,300	No tax
Over $2,300 but not over $3,400	11% of the amount over $2,300
Over $3,400 but not over $4,400	$121 + 12% of the amount over $3,400
Over $4,400 but not over $6,500	$241 + 14% of the amount over $4,400
Over $6,500 but not over $8,500	$535 + 15% of the amount over $6,500
Over $8,500 but not over $10,800	$835 + 16% of the amount over $8,500
Over $10,800 but not over $12,900	$1,203 + 18% of the amount over $10,800
Over $12,900 but not over $15,000	$1,581 + 20% of the amount over $12,900
Over $15,000 but not over $18,200	$2,001 + 23% of the amount over $15,000
Over $18,200 but not over $23,500	$2,737 + 26% of the amount over $18,200
Over $23,500 but not over $28,800	$4,115 + 30% of the amount over $23,500
Over $28,800 but not over $34,100	$5,705 + 34% of the amount over $28,800
Over $34,100 but not over $41,500	$7,507 + 38% of the amount over $34,100
Over $41,500 but not over $55,300	$10,319 + 42% of the amount over $41,500
Over $55,300 but not over $81,800	$16,115 + 48% of the amount over $55,300
Over $81,800	$28,835 + 50% of the amount over $81,800

Source: *Internal Revenue Code* Section 1, P.L. 97–34, section 101 enacted August 13, 1981

[149]

II. MARRIED TAXPAYERS FILING JOINT RETURNS

For Tax Year 1981

If taxable income is:	The tax is:
Not over $3,400	No tax
Over $3,400 but not over $5,500	14% of the amount over $3,400
Over $5,500 but not over $7,600	$294 + 16% of the amount over $5,500
Over $7,600 but not over $11,900	$630 + 18% of the amount over $7,600
Over $11,900 but not over $16,000	$1,404 + 21% of the amount over $11,900
Over $16,000 but not over $20,200	$2,265 + 24% of the amount over $16,000
Over $20,200 but not over $24,600	$3,273 + 28% of the amount over $20,200
Over $24,600 but not over $29,900	$4,505 + 32% of the amount over $24,600
Over $29,900 but not over $35,200	$6,201 + 37% of the amount over $29,900
Over $35,200 but not over $45,800	$8,162 + 43% of the amount over $35,200
Over $45,800 but not over $60,000	$12,720 + 49% of the amount over $45,800
Over $60,000 but not over $85,600	$19,678 + 54% of the amount over $60,000
Over $85,600 but not over $109,400	$33,502 + 59% of the amount over $85,600
Over $109,400 but not over $162,400	$47,544 + 64% of the amount over $109,400
Over $162,400 but not over $215,400	$81,464 + 68% of the amount over $162,400
Over $215,400	$117,504 + 70% of the amount over $215,400

For Tax Year 1982

If taxable income is:	The tax is:
Not over $3,400	No tax
Over $3,400 but not over $5,500	12% of the amount over $3,400
Over $5,500 but not over $7,600	$252 + 14% of the amount over $5,500
Over $7,600 but not over $11,900	$546 + 16% of the amount over $7,600
Over $11,900 but not over $16,000	$1,234 + 19% of the amount over $11,900
Over $16,000 but not over $20,200	$2,013 + 22% of the amount over $16,000
Over $20,200 but not over $24,600	$2,937 + 25% of the amount over $20,200
Over $24,600 but not over $29,900	$4,037 + 29% of the amount over $24,600
Over $29,900 but not over $35,200	$5,574 + 33% of the amount over $29,900
Over $35,200 but not over $45,800	$7,323 + 39% of the amount over $35,200
Over $45,800 but not over $60,000	$11,457 + 44% of the amount over $45,800
Over $60,000 but not over $85,600	$17,705 + 49% of the amount over $60,000
Over $85,600	$30,249 + 50% of the amount over $85,600

II. MARRIED TAXPAYERS FILING JOINT RETURNS *(continued)*

For Tax Year 1983

If taxable income is:	The tax is:
Not over $3,400	No tax
Over $3,400 but not over $5,500	11% of the amount over $3,400
Over $5,500 but not over $7,600	$231 + 13% of the amount over $5,500
Over $7,600 but not over $11,900	$504 + 15% of the amount over $7,600
Over $11,900 but not over $16,000	$1,149 + 17% of the amount over $11,900
Over $16,000 but not over $20,200	$1,846 + 19% of the amount over $16,000
Over $20,200 but not over $24,600	$2,644 + 23% of the amount over $20,200
Over $24,600 but not over $29,900	$3,656 + 26% of the amount over $24,600
Over $29,900 but not over $35,200	$5,034 + 30% of the amount over $29,900
Over $35,200 but not over $45,800	$6,624 + 35% of the amount over $35,200
Over $45,800 but not over $60,000	$10,334 + 40% of the amount over $45,800
Over $60,000 but not over $85,600	$16,014 + 44% of the amount over $60,000
Over $85,600 but not over $109,400	$27,278 + 48% of the amount over $85,600
Over $109,400	$38,702 + 50% of the amount over $109,400

For Tax Years After 1983

If taxable income is:	The tax is:
Not over $3,400	No tax
Over $3,400 but not over $5,500	11% of the amount over $3,400
Over $5,500 but not over $7,600	$231 + 12% of the amount over $5,500
Over $7,600 but not over $11,900	$483 + 14% of the amount over $7,600
Over $11,900 but not over $16,000	$1,085 + 16% of the amount over $11,900
Over $16,000 but not over $20,200	$1,741 + 18% of the amount over $16,000
Over $20,200 but not over $24,600	$2,497 + 22% of the amount over $20,200
Over $24,600 but not over $29,900	$3,465 + 25% of the amount over $24,600
Over $29,900 but not over $35,200	$4,790 + 28% of the amount over $29,900
Over $35,200 but not over $45,800	$6,274 + 33% of the amount over $35,200
Over $45,800 but not over $60,000	$9,772 + 38% of the amount over $45,800
Over $60,000 but not over $85,600	$15,168 + 42% of the amount over $60,000
Over $85,600 but not over $109,400	$25,920 + 45% of the amount over $85,600
Over $109,400 but not over $162,400	$36,630 + 49% of the amount over $109,400
Over $162,400	$62,600 + 50% of the amount over $162,400

Source: *Internal Revenue Code* Section 1, P.L. 97-34, section 101 enacted August 13, 1981

III. MARRIED TAXPAYERS FILING SEPARATE RETURNS

For Tax Year 1981

If taxable income is:	The tax is:
Not over $1,700	No tax
Over $1,700 but not over $2,750	14% of the amount over $1,700
Over $2,750 but not over $3,800	$147 + 16% of the amount over $2,750
Over $3,800 but not over $5,950	$315 + 18% of the amount over $3,800
Over $5,950 but not over $8,000	$702 + 21% of the amount over $5,950
Over $8,000 but not over $10,100	$1,132.50 + 24% of the amount over $8,000
Over $10,100 but not over $12,300	$1,636.50 + 28% of the amount over $10,100
Over $12,300 but not over $14,950	$2,252.50 + 32% of the amount over $12,300
Over $14,950 but not over $17,600	$3,100.50 + 37% of the amount over $14,950
Over $17,600 but not over $22,900	$4,081 + 43% of the amount over $17,600
Over $22,900 but not over $30,000	$6,360 + 49% of the amount over $22,900
Over $30,000 but not over $42,800	$9,839 + 54% of the amount over $30,000
Over $42,800 but not over $54,700	$16,751 + 59% of the amount over $42,800
Over $54,700 but not over $81,200	$23,772 + 64% of the amount over $54,700
Over $81,200 but not over $107,700	$40,732 + 68% of the amount over $81,200
Over $107,700	$58,752 + 70% of the amount over $107,700

For Tax Year 1982

If taxable income is:	The tax is:
Not over $1,700	No tax
Over $1,700 but not over $2,750	12% of the amount over $1,700
Over $2,750 but not over $3,800	$126 + 14% of the amount over $2,750
Over $3,800 but not over $5,950	$273 + 16% of the amount over $3,800
Over $5,950 but not over $8,000	$617 + 19% of the amount over $5,950
Over $8,000 but not over $10,100	$1,006 + 22% of the amount over $8,000
Over $10,100 but not over $12,300	$1,468 + 25% of the amount over $10,100
Over $12,300 but not over $14,950	$2,018 + 29% of the amount over $12,300
Over $14,950 but not over $17,600	$2,787 + 33% of the amount over $14,950
Over $17,600 but not over $22,900	$3,661 + 39% of the amount over $17,600
Over $22,900 but not over $30,000	$5,728 + 44% of the amount over $22,900
Over $30,000 but not over $42,800	$8,852 + 49% of the amount over $30,000
Over $42,800	$15,124 + 50% of the amount over $42,800

III. MARRIED TAXPAYERS FILING SEPARATE RETURNS *(continued)*

For Tax Year 1983

If taxable income is:	The tax is:
Not over $1,700	No tax
Over $1,700 but not over $2,750	11% of the amount over $1,700
Over $2,750 but not over $3,800	$115 + 13% of the amount over $2,750
Over $3,800 but not over $5,950	$252 + 15% of the amount over $3,800
Over $5,950 but not over $8,000	$574 + 17% of the amount over $5,950
Over $8,000 but not over $10,100	$923 + 19% of the amount over $8,000
Over $10,100 but not over $12,300	$1,322 + 23% of the amount over $10,100
Over $12,300 but not over $14,950	$1,828 + 26% of the amount over $12,300
Over $14,950 but not over $17,600	$2,517 + 30% of the amount over $14,950
Over $17,600 but not over $22,900	$3,312 + 35% of the amount over $17,600
Over $22,900 but not over $30,000	$5,167 + 40% of the amount over $22,900
Over $30,000 but not over $42,800	$8,007 + 44% of the amount over $30,000
Over $42,800 but not over $54,700	$13,639 + 48% of the amount over $42,800
Over $54,700	$19,351 + 50% of the amount over $54,700

For Tax Years After 1983

If taxable income is:	The tax is:
Not over $1,700	No tax
Over $1,700 but not over $2,750	11% of the amount over $1,700
Over $2,750 but not over $3,800	$115 + 12% of the amount over $2,750
Over $3,800 but not over $5,950	$241 + 14% of the amount over $3,800
Over $5,950 but not over $8,000	$542 + 16% of the amount over $5,950
Over $8,000 but not over $10,100	$870 + 18% of the amount over $8,000
Over $10,100 but not over $12,300	$1,248 + 22% of the amount over $10,100
Over $12,300 but not over $14,950	$1,732 + 25% of the amount over $12,300
Over $14,950 but not over $17,600	$2,395 + 28% of the amount over $14,950
Over $17,600 but not over $22,900	$3,137 + 33% of the amount over $17,600
Over $22,900 but not over $30,000	$4,886 + 38% of the amount over $22,900
Over $30,000 but not over $42,800	$7,584 + 42% of the amount over $30,000
Over $42,800 but not over $54,700	$12,960 + 45% of the amount over $42,800
Over $54,700 but not over $81,200	$18,315 + 49% of the amount over $54,700
Over $81,200	$31,300 + 50% of the amount over $81,200

Source: *Internal Revenue Code* Section 1, P.L. 97–34, section 101 enacted August 13, 1981

[153]

IV. UNMARRIED HEADS OF HOUSEHOLD

For Tax Year 1981

If taxable income is:	The tax is:
Not over $2,300	No tax
Over $2,300 but not over $4,400	14% of the amount over $2,300
Over $4,400 but not over $6,500	$294 + 16% of the amount over $4,400
Over $6,500 but not over $8,700	$630 + 18% of the amount over $6,500
Over $8,700 but not over $11,800	$1,026 + 22% of the amount over $8,700
Over $11,800 but not over $15,000	$1,708 + 24% of the amount over $11,800
Over $15,000 but not over $18,200	$2,476 + 26% of the amount over $15,000
Over $18,200 but not over $23,500	$3,308 + 31% of the amount over $18,200
Over $23,500 but not over $28,800	$4,951 + 36% of the amount over $23,500
Over $28,800 but not over $34,100	$6,859 + 42% of the amount over $28,800
Over $34,100 but not over $44,700	$9,085 + 46% of the amount over $34,100
Over $44,700 but not over $60,600	$13,961 + 54% of the amount over $44,700
Over $60,600 but not over $81,800	$22,547 + 59% of the amount over $60,600
Over $81,800 but not over $108,300	$35,055 + 63% of the amount over $81,800
Over $108,300 but not over $161,300	$51,750 + 68% of the amount over $108,300
Over $161,300	$87,790 + 70% of the amount over $161,300

For Tax Year 1982

If taxable income is:	The tax is:
Not over $2,300	No tax
Over $2,300 but not over $4,400	12% of the amount over $2,300
Over $4,400 but not over $6,500	$252 + 14% of the amount over $4,400
Over $6,500 but not over $8,700	$546 + 16% of the amount over $6,500
Over $8,700 but not over $11,800	$898 + 20% of the amount over $8,700
Over $11,800 but not over $15,000	$1,518 + 22% of the amount over $1,800
Over $15,000 but not over $18,200	$2,222 + 23% of the amount over $15,000
Over $18,200 but not over $23,500	$2,958 + 28% of the amount over $18,200
Over $23,500 but not over $28,800	$4,442 + 32% of the amount over $23,500
Over $28,800 but not over $34,100	$6,138 + 38% of the amount over $28,800
Over $34,100 but not over $44,700	$8,152 + 41% of the amount over $34,100
Over $44,700 but not over $60,600	$12,498 + 49% of the amount over $44,700
Over $60,600	$20,289 + 50% of the amount over $60,600

IV. UNMARRIED HEADS OF HOUSEHOLD *(continued)*

For Tax Year 1983

If taxable income is:	The tax is:
Not over $2,300	No tax
Over $2,300 but not over $4,400	11% of the amount over $2,300
Over $4,400 but not over $6,500	$231 + 13% of the amount over $4,400
Over $6,500 but not over $8,700	$504 + 15% of the amount over $6,500
Over $8,700 but not over $11,800	$834 + 18% of the amount over $8,700
Over $11,800 but not over $15,000	$1,392 + 19% of the amount over $11,800
Over $15,000 but not over $18,200	$2,000 + 21% of the amount over $15,000
Over $18,200 but not over $23,500	$2,672 + 25% of the amount over $18,200
Over $23,500 but not over $28,800	$3,997 + 29% of the amount over $23,500
Over $28,800 but not over $34,100	$5,534 + 34% of the amount over $28,800
Over $34,100 but not over $44,700	$7,336 + 37% of the amount over $34,100
Over $44,700 but not over $60,600	$11,258 + 44% of the amount over $44,700
Over $60,600 but not over $81,800	$18,254 + 48% of the amount over $60,600
Over $81,800	$28,430 + 50% of the amount over $81,800

For Tax Years After 1983

If taxable income is:	The tax is:
Not over $2,300	No tax
Over $2,300 but not over $4,400	11% of the amount over $2,300
Over $4,400 but not over $6,500	$231 + 12% of the amount over $4,400
Over $6,500 but not over $8,700	$483 + 14% of the amount over $6,500
Over $8,700 but not over $11,800	$791 + 17% of the amount over $8,700
Over $11,800 but not over $15,000	$1,318 + 18% of the amount over $11,800
Over $15,000 but not over $18,200	$1,894 + 20% of the amount over $15,000
Over $18,200 but not over $23,500	$2,534 + 24% of the amount over $18,200
Over $23,500 but not over $28,800	$3,806 + 28% of the amount over $23,500
Over $28,800 but not over $34,100	$5,290 + 32% of the amount over $28,800
Over $34,100 but not over $44,700	$6,986 + 35% of the amount over $34,100
Over $44,700 but not over $60,600	$10,696 + 42% of the amount over $44,700
Over $60,600 but not over $81,800	$17,374 + 45% of the amount over $60,600
Over $81,800 but not over $108,300	$26,914 + 48% of the amount over $81,800
Over $108,300	$39,634 + 50% of the amount over $108,300

Source: *Internal Revenue Code* Section 1, P.L. 97–34, section 101 enacted August 13, 1981

INDEX

[157]